SpringerBriefs in Law

SpringerBriefs present concise summaries of cutting-edge research and practical applications across a wide spectrum of fields. Featuring compact volumes of 50 to 125 pages, the series covers a range of content from professional to academic. Typical topics might include:

- A timely report of state-of-the art analytical techniques
- A bridge between new research results, as published in journal articles, and a contextual literature review
- A snapshot of a hot or emerging topic
- A presentation of core concepts that students must understand in order to make independent contributions

SpringerBriefs in Law showcase emerging theory, empirical research, and practical application in Law from a global author community. SpringerBriefs are characterized by fast, global electronic dissemination, standard publishing contracts, standardized manuscript preparation and formatting guidelines, and expedited production schedules.

Fabian Lutz

Practical Guide to Schengen Law

Fabian Lutz
DG Home
European Commission
Brussels, Belgium

ISSN 2192-855X   ISSN 2192-8568 (electronic)
SpringerBriefs in Law
ISBN 978-3-031-56900-5   ISBN 978-3-031-56898-5 (eBook)
https://doi.org/10.1007/978-3-031-56898-5

© The Editor(s) (if applicable) and The Author(s), under exclusive license to Springer Nature Switzerland AG 2024

This work is subject to copyright. All rights are solely and exclusively licensed by the Publisher, whether the whole or part of the material is concerned, specifically the rights of translation, reprinting, reuse of illustrations, recitation, broadcasting, reproduction on microfilms or in any other physical way, and transmission or information storage and retrieval, electronic adaptation, computer software, or by similar or dissimilar methodology now known or hereafter developed.

The use of general descriptive names, registered names, trademarks, service marks, etc. in this publication does not imply, even in the absence of a specific statement, that such names are exempt from the relevant protective laws and regulations and therefore free for general use.

The publisher, the authors and the editors are safe to assume that the advice and information in this book are believed to be true and accurate at the date of publication. Neither the publisher nor the authors or the editors give a warranty, expressed or implied, with respect to the material contained herein or for any errors or omissions that may have been made. The publisher remains neutral with regard to jurisdictional claims in published maps and institutional affiliations.

This Springer imprint is published by the registered company Springer Nature Switzerland AG
The registered company address is: Gewerbestrasse 11, 6330 Cham, Switzerland

If disposing of this product, please recycle the paper.

Foreword

It was rather unlikely that an idyllic Luxembourgish town on the river Moselle would become a household name across Europe and beyond. And yet, that is precisely what happened to the municipality of Schengen for the sole reason of its geographic proximity to where the borders of France, Germany and Luxembourg meet. At this location in 1985, representatives of the three above-mentioned states, together with Belgium and the Netherlands, signed an essentially political commitment gradually to abolish border checks. Participation of the Benelux countries was facilitated by the internal travel area they had established 25 years earlier.

One of the reasons why 'Schengen' turned into a household name are ambiguous relations with the European project, both historically and at present. Not all Member States of the European Union have abolished internal border controls amongst each other, whereas several associated countries have joined the venture. The result is an almost bewildering complexity of the legal material even experts struggle to comprehend. The *Practical Guide*, written by Fabian Lutz, provides the reader with a valuable and timely compass to chart this difficult legal terrain. In doing so, it unpacks what appears to be a paradox: the seemingly uniform 'Schengen area' is defined by underlying asymmetries from a legal perspective.

The designation of the volume as a *Practical Guide* aptly designates the essence of the contribution. Lutz is not concerned with the political assessment or a theoretical enquiry, even though a thorough understanding of historic processes defines all five chapters. His focus of attention is the legal-doctrinal conundrum of how to define the Schengen acquis, with regard to both its substantive scope (subject areas covered) and its variable geometry (participating countries). These questions will primarily be of interest for practitioners and legal academics working on one or several segments of the Schengen law. The book is by far the most comprehensive, detailed and reliable description of the topic under analysis. It deserves, as a result, to be the primary point of reference in the years to come.

Fabian Lutz is ideally placed to present readers with an authoritative statement of the scope of the Schengen law. He has worked within the European Commission's DG Home Affairs for more than two decades, thus developing an intimate knowledge of core elements of the Schengen law and the practical difficulties its demarcation can raise, notably with regard to border controls (Schengen Borders Code Regulation) and irregular migration (Carrier Sanctions Directive, Return Directive). The meticulous reconstruction of the status of all measures pertaining to the Schengen law, as well as the 'lost children' of former Schengen instruments, bears testimony to his insider knowledge of a Commission official.

At the same time, the *Practical Guide* is more than a reconstruction of the legal status quo. Lutz charts the evolution of the Schengen acquis over the past 40 years with an emphasis on the overlap and occasional tensions between inter-state cooperation and the EU institutions. In doing so, the book presents a formidable case study of how path-dependency and context-specificity define many critical areas of EU activities. There is, in other words, no master plan behind the Byzantine status quo, which, to the contrary, may reflect pure bureaucratic pragmatism. Just one example: how can we explain that some topics have never been discussed within the Schengen framework, even though they are, conceptually or practically, related to the abolition of internal border controls? National officials negotiating the original Convention Implementing the Schengen Agreement deemed it too complex and time-consuming to discuss these matters.

From a methodological perspective, the book is a doctrinal reconstruction of the legal material, which, however, goes far beyond what many other authors are doing. Lutz painstakingly demonstrates that 'desk research' can entail a veritable exercise in detective work. Throughout the chapters, he unearths documents illustrating the drafting history of specific instruments very few people are aware of, thus shedding light on the path chosen. In addition, Lutz conducted interviews with 25 'Schengen veterans' who have worked on the subject matter from the late 1980s onwards. Chapter 5 summarises the outcome of these interviews, which also inform the remainder of the book. This contemporary legal history reaffirms the idiosyncrasies of the Schengen law as a product of path-dependency. It benefited from the interdisciplinary atmosphere as an 'EU fellow' at the European University Institute in Florence. This allowed Lutz to put into writing his expertise and the outcome of scrupulous research. Anyone trying to understand the present will benefit from the *Practical Guide*.

Konstanz, Germany   Daniel Thym

Acknowledgements

The author would like to thank all those who provided input and made themselves available for research interviews. Special thanks go to Jan De Ceuster, Monika Mosshammer and Zuzana Sustr for their valuable comments. My gratitude also goes to the European Commission and the European University Institute (EUI), which facilitated the research on which this book is based by offering me a 1-year EU research fellowship.

Contents

1	**Introduction**		1
	1.1 Purpose and Structure of This Guide		1
	1.2 Schengen in a Nutshell		2
	References		6
2	**The Development of the Schengen Acquis**		7
	2.1 Historical Origins and Precedents		7
	2.2 Failed Attempts to Harmonise at EC/EU Level		8
	2.3 Successful Multilateral Cooperation Within the Emerging Schengen Frame		9
		2.3.1 Benelux Cooperation	9
		2.3.2 The 1984 Saarbrücken Agreement: An Important Trigger	10
		2.3.3 The 1985 Schengen Agreement: Defining the Policy Frame	10
		2.3.4 The 1990 Convention Implementing the Schengen Agreement: The Backbone of Schengen	11
	2.4 Consolidation of Schengen: Intergovernmental Period 1990–1999		15
		2.4.1 Elaboration of the Technical Schengen Acquis	15
		2.4.2 Preference Given by the Convention Implementing the Schengen Agreement to the Community Approach	16
		2.4.3 Fate of First Generation of "Lost Children of Schengen"	17
	2.5 Integration of Schengen into Union Law (1999): Merging the Two Worlds		19
		2.5.1 The Schengen Protocol	19
		2.5.2 Implementation of the Schengen Protocol	20
	2.6 Further Development of Schengen Acquis Within EU: From 1999 Onwards		24

		2.6.1	Static Nature of Schengen Acquis	24
		2.6.2	Council Decision 1999/437/EC	24
		2.6.3	The COREPER Approach for Determining Schengen-Relatedness	26
		2.6.4	Second Generation of "Lost Children of Schengen"	28
		2.6.5	Impact of the Entry into Force of the Lisbon Treaty	28
	2.7	Jurisprudence of the European Court of Justice on the Schengen Acquis		29
	2.8	Legal Means for Challenging the Non-labelling of a Legal act as Schengen-Related?		31
	2.9	International Agreements		31
		2.9.1	Visa and Border Management	31
		2.9.2	Readmission	32
	References			34
3	**Scope of Schengen Acquis in 2024**			**37**
	3.1	The Inner Layers		38
		3.1.1	Abolishment of Internal Border Control	38
		3.1.2	Harmonized Rules on External Borders and Visa	40
		3.1.3	Harmonized Rules on Mobility of Legally Staying Third-Country Nationals	43
		3.1.4	Large-Scale Schengen IT Systems	46
		3.1.5	Schengen Evaluation System	46
	3.2	The Outer Layers		48
		3.2.1	Document Security	48
		3.2.2	Return and Readmission	49
		3.2.3	Irregular Migration	50
		3.2.4	Police Cooperation	50
		3.2.5	Mutual Assistance in Criminal Matters	52
		3.2.6	Ne bis in idem	52
		3.2.7	Extradition	53
		3.2.8	Transfer of Enforcement of Criminal Judgments	53
		3.2.9	Drugs	54
		3.2.10	Firearms and Ammunition	54
		3.2.11	eu-Lisa	55
		3.2.12	Transport and Movement of Goods	55
		3.2.13	Data Protection	55
	3.3	The Aura		57
		3.3.1	Asylum and Immigration	58
		3.3.2	Responsibility for Processing Asylum Applications (Dublin and Eurodac)	58
		3.3.3	Free Movement Rules	59
		3.3.4	Solidarity Measures	59
		3.3.5	Responsibility Rules for Irregular Migrants	60
	References			63

4	**The Territorial Scope of Schengen**		65
	4.1	Context	65
	4.2	The Position of Ireland	65
	4.3	The Position of Denmark	69
	4.4	The Position of New Member States	72
	4.5	The Position of Cyprus	74
	4.6	The Position of Schengen Associated States	74
		4.6.1 Schengen Association Agreements	74
		4.6.2 Operation of the Agreements	75
		4.6.3 Interlinkage Between Different Schengen Association Agreements	76
		4.6.4 Interlinkage Between Schengen Association Agreements and Dublin/Eurodac Acquis	76
		4.6.5 Interlinkage Between Schengen Association Agreements and Free Movement Acquis	76
	4.7	Outermost Regions	77
		4.7.1 French and Dutch Outermost Regions	77
		4.7.2 Spanish and Portuguese Outermost Regions	77
	4.8	Microstates	77
		4.8.1 Historically Grown Practices	77
		4.8.2 Monaco	78
		4.8.3 Andorra	79
		4.8.4 San Marino	80
		4.8.5 Vatican/Holy See	80
	4.9	Faroe Islands and Greenland	80
	4.10	Foreign Military Bases	81
	4.11	UK Sovereign Base Areas of Akrotiri and Dhekelia	82
	4.12	Ceuta and Melilla	82
	4.13	Kaliningrad	83
	4.14	Mount Athos	83
	4.15	Åland Islands	84
	4.16	Svalbard (Spitzbergen)	84
	4.17	Gibraltar	84
	References		85
5	**Outcome of Research Interviews with "Schengen Veterans"**		87
6	**Conclusions**		95
	6.1	Schengen: A Success Story with an Unconventional Birth	95
	6.2	Complexity Is Impacting Legal Certainty and Policy Making	96
	6.3	Reducing Complexity by Adjusting the Scope of Schengen Law?	98

> 6.4 Or Merging the Worlds of Schengen Law and Normal EU Law?... 100
> 6.5 What Next? 101
> References... 101

Consolidated Text of the 1990 Convention Implementing the Schengen Agreement (CISA)................................. 103

Select Cases 135

Terminology... 137

Chapter 1
Introduction

1.1 Purpose and Structure of This Guide

Schengen law is legally complex and, at the same time, foundational for the free movement objectives of the European Union. This "Practical Guide to Schengen Law" seeks to explain the specific features of Schengen law and its differences from normal EU law. It focuses on the territorial scope of application of Schengen law (variable geometry) and on the determination of the substantive scope of the Schengen acquis. It also includes replies to frequently encountered practical questions arising in that field.

This guide aims to be a reference document for legal and policy experts in their daily work on Schengen-related matters. Following a brief introduction (this chapter), the guide describes the historical development of Schengen (Chap. 2), the substantive scope of the Schengen acquis as it presents itself in 2024 (Chap. 3) and the territorial scope of application of the Schengen acquis (Chap. 4). It also includes a summary of the outcome of research interviews with "Schengen veterans," i.e., officials who had worked in this field in the early days of Schengen and who could still be reached and interviewed in 2022 and 2023 (Chap. 5). The research questions posed to these veterans focused on topics on which few or no replies can be found in official documents or academic literature and included the question "Why were certain subject matters considered as Schengen-related and others not, and why has this distinction changed in the course of years?" The result of these key informant interviews facilitate understanding of the context of certain legal questions discussed in Chaps. 2, 3 and 4 of this book. In its conclusions (Chap. 6), the guide summarizes the most relevant findings and suggests possible options for reducing legal complexity in the field of Schengen law.

The author is working in the European Commission's Directorate-General Home Affairs. All views expressed in this article are purely personal and do not necessarily reflect the views of the European Commission.

© The Author(s), under exclusive license to Springer Nature Switzerland AG 2024
F. Lutz, *Practical Guide to Schengen Law*, SpringerBriefs in Law,
https://doi.org/10.1007/978-3-031-56898-5_1

The legal and factual description in these chapters is complemented by text boxes, with concrete and practical questions and answers on Schengen. A particular effort was made to provide the user with references to Schengen related data/information that cannot be easily found on the most frequently used EU legal websites (the European Union EUR-Lex website; the Court of Justice of the European Union CURIA website; the Official Journal of the European Union) and that may only be found at little known or little noticed other websites.

In addition to its descriptive function, this guide also aims at closing a gap in the scholarly analysis of Schengen. The substance of the Schengen acquis has already been subject of numerous publications, with specific emphasis on: border controls, security and human rights, institutional balance and implementation (Votoupalová, 2020, p. 407). However, there has been little scholarly attention to the challenges resulting from the application of the legal criteria, introduced in 1999, for distinguishing Schengen-related developments of the acquis from the broader Justice and Home Affairs acquis and the resulting legal and political problems.

1.2 Schengen in a Nutshell

Schengen is a brand name, derived from the name of the Luxembourgish city in which the two intergovernmental Schengen Agreements (the 1985 Schengen Agreement and the 1990 Convention Implementing the Schengen Agreement), which established an area without internal border control between participating States, were signed. When people speak about Schengen today, they normally refer to the Schengen area, characterised by the absence of internal border control and common standards applied at external borders.

The 1985 Schengen Agreement contained primarily policy statements which still had to be concretised by the 1990 Convention Implementing the Schengen Agreement. Further implementing measures (Executive Committee Decisions) were adopted in the early 1990s, based on the Convention Implementing the Schengen Agreement. Moreover, in accordance with a "Joint Declaration on Article 139" annexed to the Convention Implementing the Schengen Agreement, a verification that checks at external borders are effective had to be carried out before the Convention Implementing the Schengen Agreement could be brought into force in 1995.

Internal border control was eventually abolished in 1995 between a first group of seven Schengen States (the five signatories: Belgium, Germany, France, Luxembourg, Netherlands plus Spain and Portugal which had joined in 1991). Controls to Italy and Austria were lifted in 1998; to Greece in 2000; to Denmark, Sweden, Finland, Norway and Iceland in 2001; to Poland, Czech Republic, Slovakia, Hungary, Slovenia, Lithuania, Latvia, Estonia and Malta in 2007; to Switzerland in 2008; to Liechtenstein in 2011; and to Croatia in 2023. Internal border control to Romania and Bulgaria was lifted in 2024 (at air and sea borders; land border control remains in force pending a further Council decision to be taken in the future) and for Cyprus it was not lifted yet.

1.2 Schengen in a Nutshell

Several reasons explain, why an intergovernmental approach (and not a Community approach) was chosen in 1985 and 1990 for abandoning internal border control between Member States: On the one hand, there was, at that time, a lack of EC competence to cover most of the measures addressed in the Schengen Agreements. At the same time, the UK was opposed to an EC-wide lifting of internal border control and therefore blocked the unanimity which would have been necessary to adapt the Treaties accordingly, as well as other initiatives envisaging this objective. There was also no possibility offered by the Treaties, at that time, to proceed with closer cooperation amongst a limited number of Member States. This possibility was only created by the Amsterdam Treaty.

From the outset, the Commission had welcomed the Schengen group's initiative as a driving force and testbed for the Community for completion of the internal market (Taschner, 1997, p. 48). Evidence for the fact that Schengen was constructed as a test-laboratory for European integration and not as an intergovernmental attempt to torpedo the Community approach can be found in two important provisions of the Convention Implementing the Schengen Agreement: One which lays down the principle of the precedence of Community law in respect of the relationship between the Convention and Community instruments (Article 134 of the Convention Implementing the Schengen Agreement) and another which lays down that conventions to be concluded between *all* Member States will take precedence over the Convention Implementing the Schengen Agreement (Article 142 of the Convention Implementing the Schengen Agreement). From the very beginning, Schengen States made an effort to integrate the European Commission in its work as an observer.

Due to the success story initiated by the Schengen agreements, the name of Schengen soon became a buzzword. According to some sources, "Schengenland" is in the United States sometimes even thought to be a genuine country located somewhere in Europe (Den Boer & Corrado, 1999, p. 397). Nowadays, the use of the term Schengen most frequently relates to the geographical area (Schengen area) in which a set of rules (Schengen acquis) providing for the absence of internal border controls and flanking measures applies.

With the 1999 Amsterdam Treaty and its annexed Protocol integrating the Schengen acquis into the framework of the European Union ("Schengen Protocol"), the Schengen acquis was integrated into EC/EU law. But even after this so called "Amsterdamisation" in 1999, some reminders of the previous intergovernmental nature of Schengen law are still surviving until today, and make it different from normal Union law, namely:

1. The differing scope of its territorial application.
2. Its legal qualification as "closer cooperation" authorised by Primary law.
3. The existence of a peer review mechanism (Schengen Evaluation Mechanism).
4. The two-step approach applicable to new Member States.
5. Moreover, some legal instruments adopted before 1999 are still in force. They count as EU law, but their legal form (Convention, Executive Committee Decision) differs from the form normally used in Union law.

These Schengen specific features make it necessary to always and systematically clarify, in the recitals of each Schengen-related EC/EU legal act, that it constitutes a development of the provisions of the Schengen acquis, and to further specify the scope of its applicability having regard to the specific position of Denmark, Ireland, Norway, Iceland, Switzerland, Liechtenstein, and new Member States.

What is the "Schengen area"?
The term "Schengen area" is ambiguous. It is frequently used (incorrectly from a legal point of view) for describing the area without internal border control, made of the territories of the Schengen States already fully applying the Schengen acquis. Sometimes it is (correctly from a legal point of view) used for describing the territory of all Schengen States, including those which don't yet apply the Schengen acquis fully under the two-step procedure leading to its full application. Council made it clear in 2016 (Council document 13491/16, para. 22) that references to the "Schengen area" in official Council documents also included Bulgaria, Cyprus, and Romania. In view of this terminological ambiguity, it is advisable to always make clear in which sense the term "Schengen area" is used. Alternatively, the more precise terms: "Schengen area without internal border controls" as opposed to "territory of Schengen States" may be used, as recommended in part one of the Commissions 2022 "Practical Handbook for Border Guards" (Annex to Commission Recommendation C(2022)7591 of 28 October 2022). The legal situation has been further complicated by the adoption of Council Decision (EU) 2024/210 of 30 December 2023 on the full application of the provisions of the Schengen acquis in the Republic of Bulgaria and Romania. That Decision added a further shade of legal differentiation, since it provided for the lifting of internal border control at air and sea borders only, while the lifting of internal border control at land borders would remain in force pending a further Council decision to be taken in the future.

What is the "Schengen acquis"?
The Schengen acquis consists of a number of legal provisions which had originally evolved in an intergovernmental context, from 1985 onwards, based on the Schengen Agreements on the gradual abolition of checks at common borders signed by some Member States of the European Union in Schengen on 14 June 1985 and on 19 June 1990, as well as related rules adopted on the basis of these Agreements. In 1999, the Schengen acquis was integrated into the framework of the European Union by the Treaty of Amsterdam by means of Protocol (No 2) integrating the Schengen acquis into the framework of the European Union (1997) ("Schengen Protocol"). In accordance with Article 2 of this Protocol, Council adopted, on 20 May 1999, Decision 1999/435/EC

1.2 Schengen in a Nutshell

concerning the definition of the Schengen acquis for the purpose of determining the legal basis for each of its provisions, as well as the so-called "Ventilation Decision" 1999/436/EC, determining, in conformity with the relevant provisions of the Treaties, the EC/EU legal basis for each of the provisions or decisions which constitute the Schengen acquis. Since May 1999, proposals and initiatives building upon the Schengen acquis are subject to the relevant provisions of the Treaties.

How can I find out whether a legal act is part of the Schengen acquis?
Look at the recitals! Due to the specificities of variable geometry in the field of Schengen (position of Denmark, Ireland and the Schengen Associated States as well as the two-step procedure applicable to new Member States), any legal act building upon the Schengen acquis must be clearly indicated as such, for reasons of legal certainty. This is spelled out expressly in Article 4 of Council Decision 1999/437/EC and referred to in Recital 11 of Council Decision 1999/436/EC. The absence of Schengen recitals in a legislative act is an indication that the act was not considered, by the legislator, to be a development of the Schengen acquis.

Why was Schengen launched as intergovernmental and not as an EC project?
The reasons why an intergovernmental approach and not an EC law approach was chosen to realise the objective of abolishing internal border control between Member States can only be understood in a historical context: In the mid-1980s, a number of (continental) EC Member States were in principle open to abandon internal border control for the purpose of achieving the Single Market, but the UK preferred to keep sovereign border control, and therefore did not agree to include lifting of internal border controls in the new Article 100a EEC (qualified majority) of the 1986 Single European Act. This subject matter thus remained covered by Article 100 EEC and under unanimity requirement. Moreover, there was, at that time, a lack of EC competence to cover most of the flanking measures (visa, external border control, police and judicial cooperation) addressed in the Schengen Agreements. In the mid-1980s, EC law also did not yet provide for systems of enhanced cooperation between Member States within the EC law context. This possibility was only introduced by the Treaty of Amsterdam in 1999. Those Member States, which were willing to do so, were therefore prevented from abandoning internal border controls in an EC law context, since the UK (and Ireland which did not wish to put into question its Common Travel Area (CTA) with the UK)

would have blocked any legislation to that end under the unanimity requirement (Comte, 2017, pp. 149–151). Thus, in the 1980s, the only way in which the willing EC Member States could achieve the objective of abandoning internal border control, was to commit the "sin" of having recourse to intergovernmental cooperation. Another, complementary, explanation for the preference shown by Member States for an intergovernmental approach, was the (alleged) benefit for Member States provided by the absence of transparency requirements, the absence of involvement of EU institutions (European Parliament and Commission) and the absence of judicial control by the European Court of Justice.

References

Comte, E. (2017). *The history of the European migration regime: Germany's strategic hegemony.* Routledge.
Den Boer, M., & Corrado, L. (1999). For the record or off the record: Comments about the incorporation of Schengen into the EU. *European Journal of Migration and Law, 1*(4), 397–418.
Taschner, H. C. (1997). *Schengen: die Übereinkommen zum Abbau der Personenkontrollen an den Binnengrenzen von EU-Staaten.* Nomos-Verlag-Ges.
Votoupalová, M. (2020). Schengen cooperation: What scholars make of it. *Journal of Borderlands Studies, 35*(3), 403–423.

Chapter 2
The Development of the Schengen Acquis

2.1 Historical Origins and Precedents

The amount of "flanking measures" which need to be agreed upon to allow for the abolition of internal border checks was discussed ever since this idea became a realistic policy option at European level (Taschner, 1997, p. 12). A report on a possible Passport Union, presented in 1975 by the European Commission (COM(75)322), analysed the three regional areas without internal border control, which existed at that time in Western Europe (Benelux, Nordic Passport Union and the Common Travel Area of UK and Ireland) and concluded that it was possible to establish a free movement zone between a number of countries without necessarily adopting common policies on visa and return (only Benelux had common visa rules at that time). However, this report also found that a lack of coordination of these policies makes relevant national provisions less effective, since third-country nationals may more easily circumvent them in the absence of internal border checks.

Moreover, this report also found that abolition of internal border checks cannot be selective and apply only to EU citizens, since it is impossible—in the absence of checks—to distinguish EU citizens from third-country nationals at internal borders. The UK (supported by Ireland) declined to accept this finding and insisted that free movement should be limited to the free movement of EC/Union citizens and exclude third-country nationals, without ever providing an answer how such selective control-free movement could be implemented in practice (Taschner, 1997, p. 15). This position, which was persistently taken by UK (supported by Ireland) in the following years, blocked any proposals made by the Commission in view of adopting legally binding Conventions signed by *all* Member States or legally binding EC measures for abolishing internal border control in the period 1975–1999.

The situation in this period (1975–1999) was characterised by developments on two parallel tracks: Failed attempts to harmonise at EC/EU level (see below Sect. 2.2) and successful multilateral cooperation (see below Sects. 2.3 and 2.4) of a smaller group of Member States within the emerging Schengen frame (Schutte, 1991, pp. 562–568).

2.2 Failed Attempts to Harmonise at EC/EU Level

In 1982, the Commission proposed (COM(82)400) a first soft law measure, namely a Council Resolution on the easing of the formalities relating to checks on citizens of Member States at the Community's internal frontiers. This proposal was adopted, after 2 years of negotiations, in a watered-down form as "Resolution of Council and Governments of Member States, meeting within Council" (OJ C 159/1, 19.6.1984) and it contained four legally not binding suggestions, proposed to Member States, namely to (1) set up special checkpoints for EC/Union citizens; (2) to carry out spot-checks instead of systematic checks; (3) to consider the presentation of the passport of uniform design as basis for the presumption of belonging to a Member State; and (4) to conclude local agreements in order to make it easier for people living close to the Community's internal frontiers to cross them.

Encouraged by the political initiative of Germany and France leading to the conclusion of the July 1984 Saarbrücken agreement (see below, Sect. 2.3.2), the Commission submitted, in January 1985, a proposal for a Council Directive on the easing of controls and formalities applicable to nationals of the Member States when crossing intra-Community borders (COM(84)749). This proposal was based on an internal market legal base (Article 100 EC) and aimed at making obligatory the facilitation already mentioned in the 1984 Council Resolution. It foresaw a "principle of free passage" for EC/EU citizens at internal borders, which should be operationalised by the use of a green E-disk at land borders and the establishment of green channels (and red channels) at airports and ports. This proposal was never adopted by Council and withdrawn by the Commission in 1992 (Taschner, 1997, pp. 20–22).

As regards external border control, following the entry into force, on 1 November 1993, of the Maastricht Treaty, the Commission used its new third pillar competencies resulting from Article K and proposed, on 10 December 1993, a Council Decision establishing a Convention on controls on persons crossing external frontiers (COM(93)684). This Convention, which had already been discussed before the entry into force of the Maastricht Treaty amongst Member States in a purely intergovernmental setting, was never adopted, due to unresolvable problems related to its territorial application to Gibraltar (Zaiotti, 2011, p. 122).

In 1995, encouraged by the emerging success of the intergovernmental Schengen initiative, and pushed by the European Parliament, which had started legal action (Case C-445/93) against the Commission for alleged failure to act because it had not proposed any measure to abolish border checks by the end of 1992 (Peers, 2016, p. 73), the Commission made a new attempt, and proposed two Directives, one for a Council Directive on the elimination of controls on persons crossing internal frontiers (COM(95)347) and one for a Council Directive on the right of third-country nationals to travel in the Community (COM(95)346). The substance of these proposals was largely inspired by the Schengen acquis, which had already been developed at that time. Both proposals were based on Article 100 EC, requiring adoption by unanimity in Council, and due to the well-known position of the UK, they were never adopted.

An attempt to question the legality of internal border control through legal proceedings at the European Court of Justice also failed: In its judgment in case Wijsenbeek (C-378/97), the Court decided that Article 7a of the EC Treaty, which provided for the progressive establishment, before 31 December 1992, of an area without internal frontiers, cannot be interpreted as having direct effect, in the absence of measures adopted by the Council before 31 December 1992 requiring the Member States to abolish controls of persons at the internal frontiers of the Community. The Court underlined that abolishment of internal border control presupposes harmonisation of the laws of the Member States governing the crossing of the external borders of the Community, immigration, the grant of visas, asylum, and the exchange of information on those questions. In that context the Court stressed that, as long as Community provisions on controls at the external borders of the Community have not been adopted, the exercise of free movement rights presupposes that the person concerned is able to establish that he or she has the nationality of a Member State. The Court therefore concluded that Member States retained the right to carry out identity checks at the internal frontiers of the Community, requiring persons to present a valid identity card or passport, in order to be able to establish whether the person concerned is a national of a Member State, thus having the right to move freely within the territory of the Member States, or a national of a non-member country, not having that right.

2.3 Successful Multilateral Cooperation Within the Emerging Schengen Frame

2.3.1 *Benelux Cooperation*

Schengen was not invented from scratch. The Benelux States had already created, amongst themselves, in 1960, an area without internal borders and a common external border control and visa regime. The 1960 Benelux "Convention Concerning the Transfer of Entry and Exit Controls to the External Frontiers of the Benelux Territory" and subsequently adopted implementing Benelux rules on visa, recognised travel documents, free movement of non-Benelux nationals and specific categories of travellers, such as seamen or frontier workers, provided for a blueprint, successfully proven in practice, how an area without internal border control could also be realised within a broader European context (Turack, 1968, p. 206). As illustrated in detail in Sect. 2.3.4 below, the Benelux acquis in the field of borders and visa had a strong influence on the subsequently developed Schengen acquis.

2.3.2 The 1984 Saarbrücken Agreement: An Important Trigger

The concrete seeds for the creation of Schengen were sown in the first part of the 1980s. This was a time of crisis and institutional deadlock in European politics. It was, nonetheless, a period of political "brewing" aimed at overcoming the impasse. As had occurred in other circumstances, the Franco-German "fire" kept the Community cauldron boiling and provided a decisive impetus for change (Zaiotti, 2011, p. 67). Being aware of the difficulties for finding a solution which suited all EC Member States, the "big two" launched a bilateral political initiative for reducing controls at their bilateral border, resulting in the 13 July 1984 "Saarbrücken Agreement between France and the Federal Republic of Germany on the gradual abolition of checks at the Franco-German border". This agreement was triggered by a rather trivial event, namely a 10 day strike of French lorry drivers who were exasperated by the formalities imposed at the German borders by their own country (De Capitani, 2014, p. 104). The Saarbrücken Agreement entered into force immediately upon signature and foresaw the reduction of formalities at the borders for EC/EU citizens, which were allowed to pass through border crossing points with reduced speed, being subject to visual control without stopping and occasional spot checks only. The use of a "green disc", measuring at least 8 cm in diameter, was recommended, by which nationals of the EC Member States could indicate—to facilitate visual surveillance—that they have complied with border police rules, are carrying only goods permitted under customs rules and have complied with currency exchange regulations. As further future steps, the establishment of shared border crossing points, common visa rules, customs, and police cooperation as well as harmonised rules on migration, drugs and firearms were envisaged.

2.3.3 The 1985 Schengen Agreement: Defining the Policy Frame

In December 1984, the Benelux States asked to join the German-French Saarbrücken agreement. This led to further negotiations, resulting in the signature of the 14 June 1985 Schengen Agreement. The substance of this 1985 Schengen agreement was strongly inspired by the Saarbrücken agreement, but it was broader and more detailed. It also distinguished between "measures applicable in the short term" (Articles 1–16) and "measures applicable in the long term" (Articles 17–27). As regards controls on persons, the measures applicable in the short term focused on travel facilitation for nationals of the Member States and not yet on legally staying third-country nationals. The use of the "green disc" was recommended, just like in the Saarbrücken agreement, and the complete abolishment of checks at internal borders (this went beyond the Saarbrücken

2.3 Successful Multilateral Cooperation Within the Emerging Schengen Frame

agreement) was only defined as a measure applicable in the long term, once rules on external border control, visa, prevention of irregular migration, police and judicial cooperation and other flanking measures would have been harmonised. Despite its significant political importance, the 1985 Schengen Agreement was, to a large extent, a soft law instrument, which mainly contained recommendations as well as a work program for future harmonisation. It was subsequently concretised by the ensuing 1990 Convention Implementing the Schengen Agreement as well as new EC legislation adopted after 1985 in the field of customs and transport (where EC competence already existed and had been successfully exercised).

2.3.4 The 1990 Convention Implementing the Schengen Agreement: The Backbone of Schengen

The 1990 Convention Implementing the Schengen Agreement set out and defined, in a binding legal form, the provisions and subject matters which were henceforth referred to as Schengen acquis. The Convention Implementing the Schengen Agreement was, without any doubt, the most important legal act defining Schengen, and even though most of its provisions have been repealed and replaced in the meantime by EU/EC legal acts, its structure left its tracks in the Justice and Home Affairs legislation, and knowledge about the Convention Implementing the Schengen Agreement is important for understanding the spirit of Schengen. Or, as a former Member of the Legal Service of the Council expressed it, "the Schengen Convention is dead, but its provisions are still with us" (Huybreghts, 2015, p. 403). An informal consolidated version of the Convention Implementing the Schengen Agreement can be found in the annex to this guide. This consolidation also shows, for the purpose of historical comparison, the replaced or repealed Articles of the Convention Implementing the Schengen Agreement in shaded text.

The—compared to Benelux, Nordic Passport Union, and the Common Travel Area—relatively broad substantive scope of the 1990 Convention Implementing the Schengen Agreement was the result of intergovernmental negotiations of the five signatory States. There is no straightforward logic explanation why certain subject matters, such as firearms, drugs and "ne bis in idem", were included in the scope of the 1990 Convention Implementing the Schengen Agreement and therefore became "Schengen acquis", whilst other subject matters, which could have objectively been considered equally closely linked to the establishment of an area without internal border, such as harmonised rules on immigration, were not included. It emerged from research interviews (Chap. 5) that the determination of the scope of the Convention Implementing the Schengen Agreement was a process of negotiations in which the national interests and preferences of the five signatories played an important role.

To what extent was the text of the Convention Implementing the Schengen Agreement influenced by Benelux rules?
Major input for the substance and definition of the scope of the Convention Implementing the Schengen Agreement came from relevant Benelux rules already existing at that time (Golenvaux, 1994, p. 335). A comparison of the text of the 1960 Benelux Convention on the transfer of control of persons to the external frontiers of Benelux territory with the text of the 1990 Convention Implementing the Schengen Agreement shows several striking similarities: The distinction between short-term stays of third-country nationals, covered by harmonised rules, and long-term-stays covered by national law, which has become a guiding principle of the Schengen acquis, was already present under Benelux rules. This is set out expressly on page one of the agreed Benelux comments to the above-mentioned convention: *Dans la présente Convention, le terme « circulation des étrangers » ne vise pas un séjour de plus de trois mois dans* un des *pays du Benelux, l'établissement des étrangers continuant à être régi dans chacun des trois pays par la réglementation nationale.* As regards the entry conditions of third-country nationals for a short stay, Article 5 of the Benelux Convention follows the same line as Article 5 of the Convention Implementing the Schengen Agreement (now Article 6 of the Schengen Borders Code) : *Les étrangers en possession des documents requis et disposant de moyens de subsistance suffisants ou de la possibilité de les acquérir par un travail légalement autorisé, peuvent entrer dans le territoire du Benelux à moins qu'ils ne soient signalés comme indésirables dans ce territoire ou considérés comme pouvant compromettre la tranquillité publique, l'ordre public ou la sécurité nationale.* Article 7 of the Benelux Convention mirrors the content of Article 22 of the Convention Implementing the Schengen Agreement (reporting obligation of third-country nationals): *Les étrangers qui entrent dans un des pays du Benelux sont tenus de déclarer leur arrivée aux autorités compétentes de ce pays.* And as regards the free movement of legally staying third-country nationals, Article 8 of the Benelux Convention seems to have directly inspired the wording of Articles 19–21 of the Convention Implementing the Schengen Agreement: *Les étrangers entrés régulièrement dans le territoire du Benelux peuvent, en respectant l'obligation prévue à l'article 7 et pour autant qu'ils continuent à remplir les conditions prévues à l'article 5, circuler dans chacun des pays du Benelux pendant une durée à déterminer par le Groupe de travail. Sans préjudice de l'application de l'article 7, les étrangers porteurs d'un titre de séjour délivré dans un des pays du Benelux peuvent également circuler dans les deux autres pays du Benelux sous le seul couvert de ce document, pourvu qu'ils remplissent les autres conditions prévues à l'article 5.* Article 9 of the Benelux Convention contains the principle that undesirable third-country nationals shall be taken back by the other contracting State from which they entered. This may have influenced chapter 7 of the Convention Implementing the Schengen Agreement

2.3 Successful Multilateral Cooperation Within the Emerging Schengen Frame

dealing with responsibility for asylum seekers; Article 10 of the Benelux Convention shows similarities with Article 96 of the Convention Implementing the Schengen Agreement (entry bans); Article 11 of the Benelux Convention shows similarities with Article 23 of the Convention Implementing the Schengen Agreement (return of irregular migrants), and Article 12 of the Benelux Convention mirrors Article 2(2) of the Convention Implementing the Schengen Agreement (temporary reintroduction of internal border control for public order reasons).

As regards the field of police and judicial cooperation, another Benelux Agreement, namely the 1962 *Traité d'extradition et d'entraide judiciaire en matière pénale,* was used as source of inspiration (Elsen, 2011, p. 75): Article 27 of that Treaty contains rules on hot pursuit which show similarities with Article 41 of the Convention Implementing the Schengen Agreement and Article 8 of that Treaty contains the principle of *ne bis in idem*, also present in Article 54 of the Convention Implementing the Schengen Agreement.

The subject matters addressed by the 142 Articles of the Convention Implementing the Schengen Agreement, some of which are still in force today, were grouped in titles. At the core of the Convention Implementing the Schengen Agreement figured the title "abolition of checks at internal borders and movement of persons". It included rules on the abolition of checks at internal borders; harmonised rules on the crossing of external borders and on short-stay visas; intra-Schengen mobility of legally staying third-country nationals; reporting obligation for legally staying third-country nationals; return of illegally staying third-country nationals; conflict rules on residence permits and refusal of entry alerts; carriers liability; facilitation of illegal entry and stay and responsibility for processing applications for asylum. Next to this, the title "police and security" included rules on police cooperation; mutual assistance in criminal matters; application of the ne bis in idem principle; extradition; transfer of the enforcement of criminal judgements; narcotic drugs and firearms and ammunition. Furthermore, the Convention Implementing the Schengen Agreement included provisions on the establishment and operation of the Schengen Information System; transport and movement of goods (with the objective to facilitate movement of goods at internal borders) and data protection (as regards data communicated in application of Schengen rules).

Next to the above-mentioned topics expressly addressed by the Convention Implementing the Schengen Agreement, the abolition of internal border control presupposed, as a key element, the existence of harmonised rules on the free movement of Union citizens. Since such rules already existed, in the form of binding EEC law, at the time when the Schengen Agreements were negotiated, it was neither necessary nor legally possible to include them in the Convention Implementing the Schengen Agreement. The existence of harmonised free movement rules was, so to say, the business basis for Schengen. Any third country which wanted to be associated to Schengen (Norway, Iceland, Switzerland, and Liechtenstein) or which may wish to be associated in the future, also must accept, and apply, the EU free movement acquis beforehand, as a precondition for joining Schengen.

What is the legal fate of the 1985 Schengen Agreement?
Despite its political importance, the 1985 Schengen Agreement was qualified, already in 1999, as soft law instrument and as mere work program for future harmonisation. It had been concretised by the ensuing 1990 Convention Implementing the Schengen Agreement as well as new EC legislation adopted after 1985 in the field of customs and transport. For these reasons, Council did not assign separate EU/EC legal bases to the different Articles of the 1985 Schengen Agreement in the context of the 1999 ventilation of the Schengen acquis, but it referred, in Annex A of its Decision 1999/436/EC, *en bloc* to Article 2 of the Schengen Protocol as legal basis for the 1985 Schengen Agreement. From a formal legal perspective, the 1985 Schengen Agreement can be considered as superseded by the subsequently adopted binding rules (Picarra, 1998, p. 40).

What is the legal fate of the 1990 Convention Implementing the Schengen Agreement?
In 1999, the Schengen acquis, as it existed at that moment, including the text of the Convention Implementing the Schengen Agreement, was integrated into EC/EU law, based on the Schengen Protocol and two implementing Council Decisions (Council Decision 1999/435/EC and 1999/436/EC). The publication, in the Official Journal L 239 of 22.9.2000, of the provisions of the Convention Implementing the Schengen Agreement included all of its articles, including those for which Council had decided that they were obsolete or superseded (these were printed in italics). The Convention Implementing the Schengen Agreement was subsequently modified several times and many provisions were repealed and replaced by EU/EC legal acts, but some of its articles are still applicable today, as binding Union law. Its legal form (Convention) differs from the form normally used in Union law. Post-1999 *amendments* to the text of the Convention Implementing the Schengen Agreement were adopted in the legal form of EU/EC Regulations, Decisions or Framework Decisions. Post-1999 *replacements* of Articles of the Convention Implementing the Schengen Agreement also happened by means of EC Directives.

> **Where can I find a consolidated version of the Convention Implementing the Schengen Agreement?**
> There is no official consolidated version of the currently applicable text of the Convention Implementing the Schengen Agreement. The European Union EUR-Lex website lists the text of the Convention Implementing the Schengen Agreement and all modifying acts, but it is very cumbersome to work on that basis. An attempt to provide an updated consolidated text (reflecting the state of play in 2024) is made *in the annex to this Guide to Schengen law*. Informal consolidated versions of the Convention Implementing the Schengen Agreement are also available at the internet, such as https://en.wikisource.org/wiki/Convention_implementing_the_Schengen_Agreement (reflecting the state of play in 2013) and may be a helpful tool, but should always be cross-checked against the authentic legal acts, since these informal consolidations frequently overlook the fact that some Articles of the Convention Implementing the Schengen Agreement were repealed as regards relations between EU Member States, but still remain in force in relations between Schengen Member States and Schengen associated third-countries. Moreover, some Articles of the Convention Implementing the Schengen Agreement are formally still in place, but they were de facto superseded by the adoption of more detailed EC/EU legal instruments.

> **Where can I find a consolidated version of the Benelux rules on movement of persons and border control, as applicable in the 1970s?**
> The Benelux implementing rules are available in digital form in the Benelux Official Journal. The texts in question (as per 1 May 1978) are available, in both French and Dutch, at the Benelux website under: https://www.benelux.int/wp-content/uploads/2022/12/1978-03-96.pdf (accessed in May 2024).

2.4 Consolidation of Schengen: Intergovernmental Period 1990–1999

2.4.1 *Elaboration of the Technical Schengen Acquis*

The Convention Implementing the Schengen Agreement *entered* into force in 1993 (NB: it was only *brought* into force in March 1995, in accordance with a joint declaration on Article 139 of the Convention Implementing the Schengen Agreement). From 1993 onwards, numerous implementing measures (Executive Committee

Decisions, referred to as "SCH/Com-ex") were adopted, based on the Convention Implementing the Schengen Agreement, setting out detailed rules aimed at removing obstacles at internal borders, fixing common standard for external border control ("common manual"), common standards for issuing uniform visa ("common consular instructions"), rules on the development of the Schengen Information System, cross border police cooperation etc. These Executive Committee Decisions, together with the Articles of the Convention Implementing the Schengen Agreement, established the evolving "Schengen acquis" and their substance, as well as the philosophy behind, were to a large extent maintained, when they were replaced by EC/EU legal instruments during the early twenty-first century.

> **Where can I find a copy of the "old" Schengen acquis (i.e.: the legal acts which constituted the intergovernmental Schengen acquis in 1999)?**
> The full text of those parts of the Schengen acquis that was considered as relevant for determining an EC/EU legal base in 1999, was published in the Official Journal of the European Communities L 239 of 22.9.2000, setting out, on 473 pages, the Schengen acquis, as it stood when it was integrated into the European Union on 1 May 1999. This publication of the Schengen acquis in the Official Journal did not include those parts of the Schengen acquis for which the Council considered that it was not necessary to determine a legal basis. The latter acts are more difficult to retrieve and looking for them requires time consuming search in archives or websites.

> **Where can I find a copy of the "common manual"?—It seems this document was treated as confidential and never published**
> Contrary to the "common consular instructions," the "common manual," as listed under reference SCH/Com-ex (99)13 in annex A to Council Decision 1999/435/EC, was indeed still treated as confidential in 1999 and it was therefore not included in the publication of the Schengen acquis in the Official Journal L 239 of 22 September 2000. The Council only declassified the text of the "common manual" afterwards and it was published 2 years later in the Official Journal C 313 of 16.12.2002, pp. 97–335.

2.4.2 Preference Given by the Convention Implementing the Schengen Agreement to the Community Approach

The substantive scope of Schengen changed (and was reduced) already before the 1999 integration of the Schengen acquis into the legal framework of the EU. Articles 134 and 142 of the Convention Implementing the Schengen Agreement had given a clear priority to the Community approach: The provisions of the Convention

Implementing the Schengen Agreement should apply only in so far as they are compatible with Community law, and provisions agreed between EC Member States would take precedence. A concrete example of such "communitarisation" of the Schengen acquis was the replacement, in 1997, of chapter II/7 of the Convention Implementing the Schengen Agreement (responsibility for processing applications for asylum) by the provisions of the 1990 Dublin Convention, as set out in the 1994 "Bonn Protocol" (Sch/Com-ex (94)3) (Picarra, 1998, p. 40). Further examples include Article 4 of the Convention Implementing the Schengen Agreement (control of flight baggage) which was superseded by the Baggage Regulation (EEC) 3925/91 (see footnote 2 of Council Decision 1999/435/EC); Article 10(2) of the Convention Implementing the Schengen Agreement on a common format for visa, which was superseded by the Visa Format Regulation (EC) No 1683/95; chapter III/7 of the Convention Implementing the Schengen Agreement (firearms and ammunition) which was replaced by the Firearms Directive 91/477/EEC (see footnote 3 of Council Decision 1999/435/EC) and Title V (transport and movement of goods) the subject matter of which was covered—and therefore superseded—by EC law adopted in this field (see recital 4(d) of Council Decision 1999/435/EC).

2.4.3 Fate of First Generation of "Lost Children of Schengen"

What is the legal fate of this first generation of "lost children of Schengen"? Formally speaking these subject matters became "normal" Union law and ceased to be Schengen-related in line with the preference expressed for the Community method by Articles 134 and 142 of the Convention Implementing the Schengen Agreement. But in substance, one may argue, they remain Schengen measures, at least in a political sense, since they are intrinsically and closely linked to the logic of lifting internal borders and need to be applied in a coherent manner by all members of an area without internal border checks. The question of Schengen-relatedness had limited practical relevance until 1999, since until that moment, all Schengen States were also bound by the relevant developments of EC law, such as the Firearms Directive 91/477/EEC and the Visa Format Regulation (EC) No 1683/95 as well as Conventions agreed by *all* Member States, such as the Dublin Convention (OJ C 254, 19.8.1997) and—if it had ever been adopted—the proposed Convention on controls on persons crossing external frontiers (COM(93)684). At that time, the labelling (with Schengen recitals) of acts which had evolved within the smaller Schengen circle, and which were subsequently accepted by the larger group of all Member States, was not even a topic. On the contrary, the prevailing idea was that Schengen was a laboratory and that its rules should—in the long term—gradually be accepted by all Member States in the form of EC/EU law.

As explained in more detail in Sect. 2.6.1 below, the situation changed fundamentally from 1999 onwards. Since then, the decision whether a legal act develops the Schengen acquis or whether it is considered "normal" EU law has become very relevant for five States (Denmark, Norway, Iceland, Switzerland, and Liechtenstein) which are bound by the Schengen acquis, but not necessarily bound by "normal" EU law. It is also relevant for Ireland, and was relevant for the UK before its withdrawal from the EU. This made it vital to always distinguish clearly, when presenting and discussing initiatives on topics which are linked to Schengen, between the Schengen acquis and normal EC/EU acquis. The Amsterdam Treaty and its Schengen Protocol did not give precise indication how to deal with the first generation of "*lost children of Schengen*" and whether to still consider them, from 1999 onwards, as Schengen-related. The lack of mathematical precision (in the Schengen Protocol as well as in Schengen Association Agreements) which would have been necessary to sort out this question, led to persistent legal debates, legal uncertainty, and differing approaches. The Schengen/non-Schengen nature of Dublin was still an issue of legal debate 22 years after the integration of the Schengen acquis into the Framework of the EU (see paras 21–30 of Council Legal Service opinion on the Pact on Migration and Asylum; Council document 6357/21 and ensuing Recommendations of the Legal Services of the EP and the Council on variable geometry; Council document 5704/24).

In the course of history, some of the "lost children of the first generation" grew up and now lead an entirely independent life as "normal" EU law (such as the rules on transport and movement of goods), others still keep a link to Schengen, without being formally considered Schengen acquis (formally the Dublin acquis is not considered Schengen related, but under the Schengen Association Agreements, participation in the Dublin/Eurodac acquis is a condition for participation in the Schengen acquis) and others returned home to Schengen after having lead temporarily an independent life (the Common Format for Visa was formally reconsidered part of the Schengen acquis for the purposes of the Schengen Protocol from 2009 onwards and the Firearms Directive was formally relabelled as Schengen-related in 2017).

Why are the subject matters of visa-lists and uniform format for visa special from a Schengen perspective?
These two subject matters had already been harmonised by EC law before 1999 (Visa Format Regulation (EC) No 1683/95 and Visa List Regulation (EC) No 574/99), based on Article 100c EC and, in principle, all Member States should have remained bound by that harmonisation. Article 6 of the consolidated Denmark Protocol (No 22) expressly lists these two subject matters as an exception to the Danish opt-out and Denmark therefore takes part, until today, like any other EU Member State, in existing and new EU legislation covering that field as well as in related international agreements (visa waiver agreements). For Ireland (and the UK) there was ambiguity, as demonstrated below, whether the provision of the UK/Ireland Protocol and the possibility for a case by case opt-in under that Protocol are applicable to further developments of these two legal instruments, or whether the Schengen Protocol is applicable.

The Visa Format Regulation: In Regulation (EC) No 334/2002 amending Regulation (EC) No 1683/95 laying down a uniform format for visas, the recitals referred to the UK/Ireland Protocol (and not to the Schengen Protocol) and clarified that the UK takes part whilst Ireland does not. At the same time, reference to the Schengen Protocol was made with regard to the position of Norway and Iceland. In Regulation (EC) No 856/2008 amending Regulation (EC) No 1683/95 laying down a uniform format for visas as regards the numbering of visas, the recitals referred again to the UK/Ireland Protocol (and not to the Schengen Protocol) and clarified that the UK and Ireland don't participate. In subsequent amendments of the Visa Format Regulation in 2013, 2017 and 2023, the reference to the applicable Protocols was, however, changed, and instead of referring to the UK/Ireland Protocol, the recitals state that the Regulation constitutes a development of the provisions of the Schengen acquis in which the UK/Ireland don't participate in application of their partial Schengen participation authorised under the Schengen Protocol.

The Visa List Regulation: The recitals of Regulation (EC) No 539/2001, which replaced the Visa List Regulation (EC) No 574/1999, referred to the UK/Ireland Protocol (and not to the Schengen Protocol) as regards the position of UK and Ireland and inform that the UK and Ireland are not participating. At the same time, reference to the Schengen Protocol was made with regard to the position of Norway and Iceland. Subsequent amendments in 2003 and 2006 don't refer, in relation to UK and Ireland, to any Protocol, but simply state that UK and Ireland don't take part. From the 2009 amendment onwards, the recitals consistently state that the Regulation constitutes a development of the provisions of the Schengen acquis in which UK/Ireland don't participate under their respective partial Schengen participation under the Schengen Protocol.

The above-described facts leave open the question to what extent Ireland is, today, still bound by the old (pre-Amsterdam) versions of these legal instruments (Peers, 2016, pp. 32–33 and Council document 15698/16). It also shows that the legislator interpreted the constitutional frame governing the determination of Schengen-relatedness for the UK and Ireland differently over the course of time.

2.5 Integration of Schengen into Union Law (1999): Merging the Two Worlds

2.5.1 *The Schengen Protocol*

The intergovernmental conference preparing the Amsterdam Treaty wanted to improve both efficiency and transparency of the EUs regulatory frame. The co-existing parallel tracks of Schengen and EC/EU structures, which emerged in the 1990s, and the fact that these structures, composed frequently of identical experts, were considering the same issues in parallel in different fora, was considered as inefficient and costly. Moreover, the Schengen structures were criticised for their lack of transparency and insufficient democratic legitimacy. The Amsterdam Treaty now offered a momentum for a marriage of convenience between Schengen and the EU: Schengen could "buy in" on legitimacy while the EU could "buy in" on the successes already achieved in the Schengen context (Den Boer & Corrado, 1999, pp. 398–399). Several options for incorporation, ranging from a minimum option of authorised co-existence of two differing legal systems to a maximum option of a full merger were discussed. In the end, the intergovernmental conference preparing the Amsterdam Treaty decided to choose the maximum option of full integration of the Schengen acquis into the framework of the EU, combined with flexibility offered to the UK, Ireland, and Denmark under the relevant Protocols to the Treaty, to decide on their participation in the Schengen acquis (Zaiotti, 2011, pp. 147–153). With the entry into force of the Amsterdam Treaty, Schengen was expressly "blessed" as an authorised form of closer cooperation within the institutional and legal framework of the EU, and the Schengen acquis was formally integrated into the framework of the European Union, by means of Protocol (No 2) integrating the Schengen acquis into the framework of the European Union (1997) ("Schengen Protocol"). One may look at this solution as ending one "sin" (the intergovernmental Schengen cooperation), but committing, at the same time, another "sin", namely authorising "variable geometry" in respect of the UK, Ireland, Denmark and Schengen Associated third countries, resulting in legal complexity.

2.5.2 *Implementation of the Schengen Protocol*

In 1999, the Schengen acquis, as it existed at that moment, was integrated into Union law, based on the Schengen Protocol and two implementing Council Decisions (the Schengen Acquis Determination Decision 1999/435/EC and the Ventilation Decision 1999/436/EC). Article 2(1) of the Schengen Protocol had provided Council for that purpose with a sui generis legal base, allowing Council to decide unanimously, without need for a Commission proposal and without need for consultation of the EP (this had been labelled, in academic literature, as "*final orgy of unaccountability*") (Peers, 1999, p. 94), to determine, in conformity with the relevant provisions of the Treaties, the legal basis for each of the provisions or decisions which constitute the Schengen acquis. Based on that provision, Council defined, in Council Decision 1999/435/EC, the relevant Schengen acquis for the purpose of determining the (EU/EC) legal basis for each of its provisions, and it listed the titles and references of these legal acts in the annexes to that decision. Article 1(2) of Council Decision 1999/435/EC also created a legal basis for publishing the full text of the relevant Schengen acquis in the Official Journal of the European Communities. This publication took place more than 1 year afterwards, in the Official Journal L 239 of 22.9.2000, setting out, on 473 pages, the Schengen acquis, as it stood when it was integrated into the European Union on 1 May 1999.

The publication of the Schengen acquis in the Official Journal did not include those parts of the Schengen acquis for which the Council considered that it was not necessary to determine a legal basis. Recital 4 of Decision 1999/435/EC

2.5 Integration of Schengen into Union Law (1999): Merging the Two Worlds

enumerated six grounds, based on which it was justified for the Council to conclude that it is not necessary or appropriate to determine a legal basis, in conformity with the relevant provisions of the Treaties:

(a) The provision does not have any binding legal force, and a comparable provision can be adopted by the Council only on the basis of an instrument that has no legal basis in one of the Treaties.
(b) The passage of time and/or events have rendered the provision redundant.
(c) The provision relates to institutional rules which are regarded as being superseded by European Union procedures.
(d) The subject matter of the provision is covered by—and therefore superseded by—existing European Community or Union legislation or by a legal act adopted by all Member States.
(e) The provision has been made redundant by the Agreement to be concluded with the Republic of Iceland and the Kingdom of Norway pursuant to Article 6 of the Schengen Protocol.
(f) The provision concerns an area covered neither by the activity of the Community nor by the aims of the European Union and thus concerns one of those areas in which the Member States have retained freedom to act. This includes provisions which may be significant only for the purposes of calculating financial claims of or between the Member States concerned.

In some, but not in all cases, express explanations for the non-inclusion of certain legal acts, based on the above-mentioned six reasons, were given in footnotes to the annexes of Decision 1999/435/EC. The publication, in the Official Journal, of the provisions of the Convention Implementing the Schengen Agreement itself included all its articles, including those for which Council had decided that a legal basis does not need to be determined (for one of the reasons mentioned above), and the latter were printed in italics. The legal acts were grouped according to subject matter. To that end, the Schengen acquis was classified into: horizontal issues; the abolition of checks at internal borders and the free movement of persons; police cooperation; judicial cooperation in criminal matters; and the Schengen Information System.

With the simultaneously adopted Ventilation Decision 1999/436/EC determining, in conformity with the relevant provisions of the Treaty establishing the European Community and the Treaty on European Union, the legal basis for each of the provisions or decisions which constitute the Schengen acquis, Council assigned an EU/EC legal basis for each part of the Schengen acquis which had been listed in Decision 1999/435/EC.

What was the difference between an "EU legal basis" and an "EC legal basis"?
The provisions of the Schengen acquis had to be split up into those which were covered by the "third pillar" legal basis of Title VI of the EU Treaty (provisions on police and judicial cooperation in criminal matters) and those covered by a "first pillar" legal basis. In most cases the "first pillar" legal basis

was Part Three, Title IV of the EC Treaty (visas, asylum, immigration, and other policies related to free movement of persons). This distinction between an EU and an EC legal basis was abandoned with the entry into force of the Lisbon Treaty on 1.12.2009.

Could UK, Ireland and Denmark participate—between 1999 and 2009—in the adoption of third pillar legal instruments?
Yes. Both the UK/Ireland Protocol (No 4) and the Denmark Protocol (No 5) left unaffected the participation of these three States in the field of Title VI of the EU Treaty. This implied that these States could participate in the adoption of third-pillar instruments (such as the European Arrest Warrant Framework Decision 2002/584/JHA, the Prüm II Framework Decision 2008/615/JHA or the Europol Decision 2009/371/JHA) and that they were bound by these instruments like any other Member State.

Could UK, Ireland and Denmark participate—between 1999 and 2009—in the adoption of *Schengen-related* third pillar legal instruments?
On that aspect, the Schengen Protocol (No 2) foresaw that UK and Ireland could not participate, unless the instrument fell into the scope of the authorised partial Schengen participation of UK or Ireland. For Denmark the situation was different: The Denmark Protocol (No 5) including its special rules on initiatives building upon the Schengen acquis, applied only to first pillar/EC measures. Denmark could participate, until 2009, in the adoption of Schengen related third pillar legal instruments like any other Member State.

Could UK, Ireland and Denmark participate—between 1999 and 2009—in the adoption of first pillar instruments under Title IV of the EC Treaty (visas, asylum, immigration and other)?
The UK/Ireland Protocol (No 4) provided a possibility for UK and Ireland to exercise a case-by-case opt in. The Denmark Protocol (No 5) excluded Denmark from participation as a rule (subject to a limited exception under Article 4 of that Protocol).

2.5 Integration of Schengen into Union Law (1999): Merging the Two Worlds

Could UK, Ireland and Denmark participate—between 1999 and 2009—in the adoption of *Schengen-related* **first pillar instruments under Title IV of the EC Treaty (visas, asylum, immigration and other)?**
On that aspect, the Schengen Protocol (No 2) foresaw that UK and Ireland could not participate, unless the instrument fell into the scope of the authorised partial Schengen participation of UK or Ireland. For Denmark the situation was different: Under the Denmark Protocol (No 5) it could never participate in the adoption of first pillar legal instrument (Schengen related or not), but Article 5 of the Denmark Protocol (No 5) allowed Denmark to implement first pillar Schengen-related legal instrument in its national law and to be bound via an international law obligation.

Council Decision 1999/436/EC mentions, in its recitals, that future proposals amending or building upon the Schengen acquis shall be subject to the relevant provisions of the Treaties, including those governing the form of the act (recital 3), and it highlights the need for adding Schengen recitals so that legal certainty is guaranteed and the provisions related to the Schengen Protocol can be applied in every case (recital 11). An obligation to add Schengen recitals is also expressly prescribed in Article 4 of Council Decision 1999/437/EC on the arrangement for the application of the Norway/Iceland Schengen Association Agreement.

Are Schengen recitals constitutive or declaratory for the Schengen/ non-Schengen relatedness of a legislative act?
No straightforward answer to this question can be found in existing legislation or case law. In the light of the principles of rule of law and legal certainty, there are convincing arguments for considering the existence of Schengen recitals as constitutive and not merely declaratory. It can be assumed that the European Court of Justice, if it were ever confronted with that question, would probably confirm that a clear designation of Schengen relatedness is required in each Schengen act, given the relevance of such labelling for its scope of territorial application and the applicable decision-making procedure.

Should delegated or implementing acts also contain Schengen recitals?
As regards delegated and implementing acts, one may argue that they automatically share the Schengen or non-Schengen-relatedness of the legislative act on which they are based. Schengen recitals in delegated or implementing may therefore be considered as declaratory and not constitutive, even though it is highly advisable to include them since, in administrative practice, the presence of a Schengen recital is the main trigger for notifying an act to Schengen Associated States under the relevant provisions of the Schengen Association Agreements.

2.6 Further Development of Schengen Acquis Within EU: From 1999 Onwards

2.6.1 Static Nature of Schengen Acquis

From 1999 onwards, the scope of the Schengen acquis should have remained static, due to the Schengen Protocol and the Denmark Protocol as well as the Schengen Association Agreements, which all foresaw a "freezing" of the subject matters considered as Schengen-related as they were in 1999 or upon conclusion of the Association Agreements. However, in practice, this was not always the case, thanks to a restrictive approach taken by the legislator from 1999 onwards, when it came to defining the Schengen-relatedness of further developments of the Justice and Home Affairs acquis on subject matters, such as police and judicial cooperation, which had been considered as Schengen related when integrating the Schengen acquis into Union law.

2.6.2 Council Decision 1999/437/EC

In its Decision 1999/437/EC which was, like the Schengen Acquis Determination Decision 1999/435/EC and the Ventilation Decision 1999/436/EC, adopted without corresponding Commission proposal, without consultation of the EP and directly based on Article 2(1) of the Schengen Protocol, Council defined the areas in which the further development of the existing Schengen acquis will be considered as Schengen-related for the purposes of the Norway/Iceland Schengen Association Agreement. This list, which was subsequently also used as the relevant legal frame for determining Schengen-relatedness in general, going beyond that Association Agreement and for purposes of the Schengen Protocol, enumerates the following areas in which the further development of Union law will be considered as Schengen-related (bold and italics added by author):

(A). The crossing by persons of the **external borders** of those States which have decided to abolish checks at their internal borders, including the rules and arrangements with which those States must comply when carrying out checks on persons at external borders, surveillance of border areas and cooperation with the services responsible for border control.

(B). **Short-stay visas**, particularly the rules on a uniform visa, the list of countries whose nationals must be in possession of visas for the States concerned and those whose nationals are exempt from that requirement, the procedures, and conditions for the issue of uniform visas, and cooperation and consultation between the issuing services.

2.6 Further Development of Schengen Acquis Within EU: From 1999 Onwards

(C). **Free movement, for a maximum period of 3 months**, of nationals of third countries within the territory of those States which have decided to abolish checks at their internal borders and expulsion of such persons when their position is illegal.

(D). The **settlement of disputes** between States in cases where a State has issued or is considering issuing a residence permit to an alien reported as a person not to be permitted entry by another State.

(E). The penalties applicable to **carriers** and those responsible for organising **illegal immigration**.

(F). **Protection of personal data** exchanged between the services referred to in points A and B.

(G). The **Schengen Information System (SIS),** including the relevant provisions on protection and security of data, the provisions on the operation of the national sections of the SIS and the exchange of information between those national sections (SIRENE system), and the effect of the alerts in the SIS for persons wanted for arrest for extradition purposes.

(H). Any form of **police cooperation** coming under Articles 39–43, 46, 47, 73 and 126 to 130 of the Convention of 19 June 1990 implementing the Schengen Agreement on the gradual abolition of checks at the common borders, *as applied between the Member States concerned at the time of entry into force of the Treaty of Amsterdam.*

(I). The arrangements for **judicial cooperation** in criminal matters described in Articles 48–63 and 65–69 of the 1990 Convention referred to in point H, *as applied between the Member States concerned at the time of the entry into force of the Treaty of Amsterdam.*

Decision 1999/437/EC raises several legal questions: *Firstly*, it had been adopted based on Article 2 of the Schengen Protocol, which mandated the Council to take any necessary measure for defining the Schengen acquis, for determining appropriate legal bases and for integrating it into the framework of the European Union. Article 2 did not provide an express legal basis to fix rules concerning the future application of Schengen Association Agreements. It can therefore be argued that this decision lacked an appropriate legal basis. *Secondly*, this decision constituted a unilateral decision by the EU to narrow the scope of the Norway/Iceland Schengen Association Agreement which, according to its Article 2(3), had envisaged to cover all measures taken by the European Union amending or building upon the Schengen acquis listed in the annexes to that agreement, without limiting such developments to the areas enumerated in lit A-I and without the standstill clause "as applied between the Member States concerned at the time of entry into force of the Treaty of Amsterdam" introduced by Council in lit H and I (Bracke et al., 2002, p. 31). *Thirdly* the list of areas appears incomplete, since it does not include certain subject matters which were subsequently considered as Schengen-related for the purposes of the Schengen Association Agreements, such as return or firearms.

2.6.3 The COREPER Approach for Determining Schengen-Relatedness

In the years following 1999, the scope of the Schengen acquis, labelled as such by Schengen recitals (NB: as already mentioned above in Sect. 2.5.2, the existence of Schengen recitals is the only objective and measurable indicator of formal Schengen-relatedness), was further reduced, creating a second generation of *"lost children of Schengen"*. It emerged from research interviews (Chap. 5) that this development was mainly driven by policy considerations, such as offering the UK a possibility to participate and/or to avoid having third countries (Schengen Associated States) too much involved in EU internal decision-making. In many cases, the Commission proposals had foreseen Schengen-relatedness of the proposed legal acts, but this was contested and changed by Council, which stringently applied a rather restrictive approach on Schengen-relatedness set out by COREPER in 1999 (Council document 12164/99, titled "How to decide whether a particular subject matter is "Schengen-related" and must be dealt with through "Mixed Committee" procedure"). Formally this document only dealt with Schengen-relatedness for the purpose of the Norway/Iceland Schengen Association Agreement, but it was de facto also applied for determining Schengen-relatedness for the purpose of the Schengen Protocol and resulting consequences for UK and Ireland. Council itself made, for instance, express references to both the situation of UK/Ireland and Norway/Iceland in para 5 of Council doc 12503/01 on the Schengen-relatedness of the European Arrest Warrant. The official justification given by Council for its restrictive Schengen-relatedness approach was the argument that the principle of mutual recognition, on which many of the post-Tampere initiatives in the field of police and judicial cooperation were based, was qualitatively different from the mere cooperation set out in the Convention Implementing the Schengen Agreement. According to this Council doctrine, acts based on mutual recognition therefore constituted an *aliud* and could not be considered a development of the Schengen acquis, even if they clearly covered subject matters previously regulated by the Convention Implementing the Schengen Agreement. Moreover, Council took the view that new acts should only be labelled Schengen-related if they were *essential* in terms of the realization of the objectives of Schengen. This line was consistently applied, see for instance the Council documents on the Schengen-relatedness of the European Evidence Warrant (documents 10665/04 and 11415/04), the European Investigation Order (document 13514/10), the Police Cooperation part of the Internal Security Fund (document 5250/12) and the General Data Protection Regulation (document 12682/12). The distinction made in these Council Legal Service opinions between acts which are "essential" or only "desirable" cannot be found anywhere in the Schengen Protocol or in the Schengen Association Agreements. It rather seems to stem from work carried out by EU Member States in the early days of intergovernmental JHA cooperation: The 1989 "Palma Document - Free Movement of Persons, A Report to the European Council by the Coordinators' Group" (this document was never officially published, but its full text is available in Bunyan, 1997, pp. 12–16), had provided a work programme with lists of "essential" and "desirable" measures concerning the realisation of free movement of persons, with the aim of realising

2.6 Further Development of Schengen Acquis Within EU: From 1999 Onwards

within the Community (and not the Schengen) frame the objective of establishing, by 31 December 1992, an area without internal frontiers.

The COREPER Approach for Determining Schengen-Relatedness
Extract from Council document 12164/99—*How to decide whether a particular subject matter is "Schengen-related" and has to be dealt with through "Mixed Committee" procedures?* (underlining and bold taken from original document)

(...) 3. It is clear from the text of the Agreement *(comment: the Norway/Iceland Schengen Association Agreement)* and its negotiating history that it is up to the Union, and the Union alone, to determine which proposed acts or measures purport to amend or modify the provisions of the Schengen acquis listed in the Annexes to the Agreement. Of course, the Union has to apply the Agreement in good faith and delegations of Iceland and Norway in the Mixed Committee may always raise questions as to the way in which the Union interprets and applies the Agreement.

4. For the purposes of determining in advance in which areas legislative proposals would constitute acts building upon the Schengen acquis to which the procedures of Article 4 of the Association Agreement with Iceland and Norway would have to be applied, the Council has adopted its Decision of 17 May 1999 (1999/437/EC) in which it has listed a number of relevant areas. The description of these areas inevitably leaves room for divergent interpretation. This is the case in particular with respect to the areas of "police co-operation" and "judicial co-operation in criminal matters" (including drugs related matters) as well as some Title IV issues, where the Schengen acquis constitutes a limited set of rules, which do not cover the whole range of possible co-operation.

(…) 8. … In considering the possible "Schengen relevance" of a proposal or initiative it should be clear that it falls within the terms of the provisions of the Protocol integrating the Schengen acquis into the framework of the European Union. If so, the main test for determining whether a particular proposal or initiative should be considered as "Schengen-related" could be the following: **Does this proposal or initiative concern a matter which is essential to the free movement of persons within an area where checks on persons at internal borders have been eliminated and a common system of control on at the external borders has been set up and by which Iceland and Norway therefore should be bound?** The mere fact that it would be *desirable* or *practical* if Iceland and Norway were also bound would not be sufficient to apply the association procedures. It should be *essential* in terms of the realization of the objectives of Schengen co-operation: abolition of checks on persons at internal borders and the taking of inevitable and essential flanking measures in the interest of immigration control, public order and internal security. In other words: the association with Iceland and Norway serves the narrow objective of establishing an *area of free movement of persons* (for third-country nationals for periods up to 3 months), as distinct from the much wider substantive objective of the Union in the field of Justice and Home Affairs, i.e. the *creation of an area of freedom, security and justice.* (…)

2.6.4 Second Generation of "Lost Children of Schengen"

Consequently, several subject matters, mainly in the field of police and judicial cooperation, ceased to be considered Schengen-related or are now split into Schengen and non-Schengen-related parts, creating a second generation of *"lost children of Schengen"*. Denmark (under the terms of its self-imposed Protocol) and the four Schengen Associated States were thereby excluded from the application of further developments in these parts of the acquis and had to be brought in again, where this was considered desirable, through separate agreements and arrangements covering relations with Europol, Eurojust, Prüm, mutual legal assistance, extradition and the Dublin/Eurodac acquis. A straightforward labelling of these legal acts as Schengen-related would have avoided the need for such detour.

This development lead, overall, to a very complex legal situation. Uncertainty as to which Articles of the Convention Implementing the Schengen Agreement have been repealed, replaced, superseded, or remained partially applicable (in relations between Member States and Schengen Associated States but not between Member States themselves) explain why there is currently (in May 2024) no official consolidated version of the Convention Implementing the Schengen Agreement available at the European Union EUR-Lex website. This situation is very deplorable from a legal certainty angle.

2.6.5 Impact of the Entry into Force of the Lisbon Treaty

The Lisbon Treaty entered into force on 1.12.2009. From a Schengen perspective, the most important change it brought about was the abolishment of the previous third-pillar legal basis of Title VI of the EU Treaty (provisions on police and judicial cooperation in criminal matters) and its integration into the new "first pillar" legal basis of Part Three, Title V TFEU (area of freedom, security, and justice). This Treaty change and the resulting adaptations to the Protocols foresaw a continued application of the previously adopted third-pillar instruments (such as the European Arrest Warrant Framework Decision 2002/584/JHA, the Prüm II Framework Decision 2008/615/JHA or the Europol Decision 2009/371/JHA) to the UK, Ireland, and Denmark. For post-Lisbon amendments to these instruments or new initiatives in these fields, the "normal" rules applicable to first pillar instruments became applicable. This had an important impact for Denmark which was thereby excluded (under the self-imposed limitations of the Denmark Protocol) from participating in post-Lisbon developments in the field of police and judicial cooperation unless these constitute a development of the Schengen acquis. In the latter case Denmark may implement these new rules in its national law and it is bound via an international law obligation. For Ireland (and previously the UK) the effect was more limited, due to the opt-in option under the UK/Ireland Protocol (No 21).

> **Can Ireland and Denmark participate, since 2009, in the adoption of legal instruments in previous "third pillar" fields (provisions on police and judicial cooperation)?**
> The UK/Ireland Protocol (No 21) provides a possibility for Ireland to exercise a case-by-case opt in. The Denmark Protocol (No 22) excludes Denmark from participation as a rule (subject to a limited exception under Article 6 of that Protocol)

> **Can Ireland and Denmark participate, since 2009, in the adoption of** *Schengen-related* **legal instruments in previous "third pillar" fields (provisions on police and judicial cooperation)?**
> On that aspect, the Schengen Protocol provides that Ireland cannot participate, unless the instrument falls into the scope of the partial Schengen participation of Ireland. For Denmark the situation is different: Under the Denmark Protocol (No 22) Denmark can never participate in the adoption of legal instruments based on Part Three, Title V TFEU (Schengen related or not), but Article 4 of the Denmark Protocol (No 22) allows Denmark to implement first pillar Schengen-related legal instrument in its national law and to be bound via an international law obligation.

2.7 Jurisprudence of the European Court of Justice on the Schengen Acquis

The above-described legal uncertainty on the exact scope of the Schengen acquis is in contrast with the jurisprudence which the European Court of Justice had developed in three judgements related to the UKs wish to take part in acts of the Schengen acquis outside the scope of UKs authorised partial Schengen participation (Cases C-77/05, C-137/05 and C-482/08). In these cases, the Court emphasised that, when classifying a measure as falling within an area of the Schengen acquis or as a development of that acquis, the need for coherence of that acquis, and the need—where that acquis evolves—to maintain that coherence, must be taken into account (C-482/08, para 48). The Court stated that, like the choice of the legal basis of a Community act, the classification of a measure as developing the provisions of the Schengen acquis had a direct effect on the determination of the provisions governing the procedure for the adoption of that act (C-77/05, para 75), and that in analogy with what applies in relation to the choice of the legal basis of a Community act, the classification of a Community act as a proposal or initiative to build upon the Schengen acquis must rest on objective factors which are amenable to judicial review, including in particular the aim and the content of the act (C-77/05, para 77). The Court also emphasised, that the question of the legal basis of an act and the question of its Schengen-relatedness are separate (C-482/08, para 64). There is therefore no automatic link between the choice of a certain legal basis in the Treaty and the Schengen-relatedness of an act, and no such thing as a "Schengen legal basis". The Court underlined that the coherence of the Schengen acquis means that the participating States, when they develop it and deepen the closer cooperation which they have been authorised to establish by the Schengen Protocol, are not obliged to provide for special adaptation measures for the non-participating Member States (C-482/08, para 49). This statement by the Court does not seem to be fully in line with what had happened in practice from 1999 onwards, when many of the post-Tampere initiatives in the field of police and judicial cooperation were deliberately labelled as non-Schengen-related in order to allow the non-Schengen Member States UK and Ireland to participate.

In its submission in case C-482/08, referred to in para 39 of the judgement, Council expressly referred to Council Decision 1999/437/EC (setting out the criteria for determining Schengen-relatedness in the context of the Norway/Iceland Schengen Association Agreement) as the relevant legal frame for determining Schengen-relatedness in general, going beyond that Association Agreement and including for the purposes of the Schengen Protocol. The Court seemed to follow that approach: In an obiter dictum (para 58 of judgment in case C-482/08), it made clear that there is just one concept of Schengen-relatedness both for the purpose of the Schengen Protocol and for the purpose of the Schengen Association Agreements. Based on this judgment it seems therefore not possible to consider a legal act, at the same time, as not Schengen-related for UK/Ireland but as Schengen-related for Norway, Iceland, or Switzerland.

Is there a "Schengen legal basis"?
No. There is no linkage between the use of a certain legal basis in the Treaties and the Schengen-relatedness of a legal act. Whereas the choice of the legal basis for an act must be based on the provisions of the Treaties which confers on the European Union institutions the power to adopt that measure, the Schengen-relatedness of an act must be determined according to different criteria, namely whether the measure builds upon the substance of the Schengen *acquis* within the meaning of the Schengen Protocol. This was expressly confirmed by the European Court of Justice in para 64 of its judgment in case C-482/08: "*However, the question whether a measure constitutes a development of the Schengen acquis is separate from that of the legal basis on which that development must be founded.*"

> **Are there different concepts of "Schengen relatedness"?**
> No. The European Court of Justice made clear that there is just one concept of Schengen-relatedness both for the purpose of the Schengen Protocol and for the purpose of the Schengen Association Agreements. Based on this judgment it seems therefore not possible to consider a legal act, at the same time, as not Schengen-related for UK/Ireland but as Schengen-related for Norway, Iceland, or Switzerland.

2.8 Legal Means for Challenging the Non-labelling of a Legal act as Schengen-Related?

The question arises, why States directly affected by the non-labelling of a legal act as Schengen-related, such as Norway, Iceland, Switzerland, or Denmark, never challenged such a decision at the European Court of Justice.

As regards Denmark, this may be explained by the fact that Denmark could still take part, until 2009, in the adoption of third pillar JHA instruments covering the policy fields of police and judicial cooperation, and that the revised Denmark Protocol allowed Denmark to continue applying these also after 2009. Denmark was therefore not excluded from these instruments. It may, however, gradually become excluded in the future as these instruments develop further and change in substance, and therefore may not be covered any more by the "continuation" clause of Article 2 of the Protocol on the position of Denmark as amended by the Lisbon Treaty. It must also be highlighted that the abovementioned "exclusion" of Denmark is self-imposed and that Denmark may, at any time, avail itself of the options under either Article 7 or Article 8 of the Denmark Protocol to participate more broadly in the EUs freedom, security and justice acquis.

As regards the Schengen Associated States themselves, they had no standing to bring a case to the European Court of Justice. They could only raise the issue at Mixed Committee level and in public statements, which they also sometimes did, but without success (Filliez et al., 2008, pp. 176–177; Wichmann, 2006, p. 104).

Ireland, and previously UK, also had no reason to oppose the non-labelling of a legal act as Schengen -related, since they could opt in or opt out under the UK/Ireland Protocol into any non-Schengen-related JHA act.

2.9 International Agreements

2.9.1 Visa and Border Management

In several policy fields falling within the scope of the Schengen acquis or related to that acquis, the EU concludes international agreements complementing its internal (Schengen) policies. This is the case in the field of visa (visa waiver agreements and visa facilitation agreement) and in the field of integrated border management (Frontex status agreements with third countries). Denmark, though a Member State, applies the Schengen acquis only under international law, and is therefore not directly bound by international agreements concluded by the EC/EU in this field. The same is also true for Norway, Iceland, Switzerland, and Liechtenstein (sovereignty of Schengen Associated States in external relations). However, this does not mean that these countries may freely conclude international agreements affecting the Schengen acquis. Article 136(2) of the Convention Implementing the Schengen Agreement provides that no Party shall conclude international agreements with third countries simplifying or abolishing border checks. This provision illustrates the need for a common (Schengen) external policy in all matters governed by the Schengen acquis and the underlying principles does not merely apply to border controls, but to all matters governed by the Schengen acquis, including the issuing of Schengen visa (Martenczuk, 2008, p. 520). It implies that Denmark and the Schengen Associated States are not free to negotiate visa agreements derogating from the common Schengen rules. Likewise, where the EC/EU has concluded an international agreement, it will be necessary that these States conclude similar agreements. In practice, at the occasion of the conclusion of such EU agreements with a third country, a declaration is made, calling for the conclusion of parallel agreements with Denmark and the Schengen Associated States.

As regards Denmark, there is, however, one important exception to this rule: Due to a special derogation in Article 6 of the Protocol on the position of Denmark as amended by the Lisbon Treaty, the Danish opt-out does not apply to measures determining the third countries whose nationals must be in a possession of a visa when crossing the external borders of the Member States. Denmark therefore participates directly in visa waiver agreements (which regulate visa obligations) as a normal Member State. But it does not participate in visa facilitation agreements since these agreements address visa issuing procedures and not visa obligations.

As regards Ireland (and previously UK) it is not part of the Schengen area and for as long as its Schengen participation does not extend to the area covered by the international agreement, it is free to conduct its own external policy in the field of external borders and visa..

2.9.2 Readmission

For readmission the situation is different: Even though both return and readmission had originally constituted a part of the Schengen acquis (readmission was mentioned in Article 23(4) of the Convention Implementing the Schengen Agreement and "policy on expulsion and readmission" was listed in the 1998 Executive Committee Decision setting up Schengen Evaluation (SCH/Com-ex (98)26 def),

2.9 International Agreements

moreover two Schengen Acts expressly dealt with readmission related challenges, namely the Executive Committee Decision on the guiding principles for means of proof and indicative evidence within the framework of readmission agreements between Schengen States (SCH/Com-ex (97)39 rev.) and the Executive Committee Decision on measures to be taken in respect of countries posing problems with regard to the issue of documents required for expulsion from the Schengen territory (SCH/Com-ex (98)18 rev.)) Council decided, from 2000 onwards, to consider readmission agreements as a non-Schengen-related matter (Papagianni, 2006, p. 54). As a consequence the UK/Ireland Protocol was applied to readmission agreements and not—like for visa waiver and visa facilitation agreements—the Schengen Protocol.

Both the UK and Ireland benefitted from that opportunity and were allowed to choose to opt in or out of these agreements on a case-by-case basis (Schieffer, 2008, pp. 104–106). Denmark, in application of its Protocol, could not take part. The Schengen Associated States were also not bound by readmission agreements concluded between the EC/EU and a third country. This raised an issue from the Schengen perspective of a coherent return and readmission policy, given the possibility for irregular migrants to move between Schengen States without being subject internal border checks. Consequently, on the occasion of the conclusion of all readmission agreements, declarations were issued which called for the conclusion of parallel readmission agreements between Denmark, Norway, Iceland, Switzerland, Liechtenstein and the third countries concerned (Martenczuk, 2008, p. 521).

Which EU/Schengen States are bound by EU visa facilitation agreements?
25 EU Member States (all Member States except Ireland and Denmark) are directly bound. Ireland is not bound and cannot participate (neither under the Ireland/UK Protocol since the visa policy is considered Schengen-related; nor under the Schengen Protocol, since visa policy is not covered by the Irish partial Schengen participation). Denmark is not bound, but given its Schengen participation under Article 4 of the Denmark Protocol, a joint declaration should be made, calling for a parallel agreement. The Schengen Associated States are not bound, but given their Schengen Association, a joint declaration should be made, calling for parallel agreements.

Which EU/Schengen States are bound by EU visa waiver agreements?
Same as above, but with the difference that Denmark is directly bound as a Member States, due to the derogation in Article 6 of the Denmark Protocol.

Which EU/Schengen States are bound by EU Frontex status agreements?
25 EU Member States (all Member States except Ireland and Denmark) are directly bound. Ireland is not bound and cannot participate (neither under the Ireland/UK Protocol since Frontex is considered Schengen-related; nor under the Schengen Protocol, since Frontex is not covered by the Irish partial Schengen participation). Denmark is not bound, but given its Schengen participation under Article 4 of the Denmark Protocol, a joint declaration should be made calling for a parallel agreement. The Schengen Associated States are not bound, but given their Schengen Association, a joint declaration should be made, calling for parallel agreements.

Which EU/Schengen States are bound by EU readmission agreements?
25 EU Member States (all Member States except Ireland and Denmark) are directly bound. Ireland is free to opt in on a case-by-case basis under the Ireland/UK Protocol, since readmission is not considered as Schengen-related. Denmark is not bound but given the close political connection of readmission to Schengen, a joint declaration may be made calling for a parallel agreement. The Schengen Associated States are not bound but given the close political connection of readmission to Schengen, a joint declaration may be made, calling for parallel agreements.

References

Bracke, N., Cullen, P. J., & Jund, S. (2002). The Amsterdam Treaty Framework with special reference to the incorporation of the Schengen Acquis. In P. Cullen & S. Jund (Hgs.), *Criminal justice co-operation in the European Union after Tampere* (pp. 23–34). Bundesanzeiger.

Bunyan, T. (1997). Key texts on justice and home affairs in the European Union from Trevi to Maastricht (Vol. 1) (1976–1993).

De Capitani, E. (2014). The Schengen system after Lisbon: From cooperation to integration. *ERA Forum, 15*(1), 101–118.

Den Boer, M., & Corrado, L. (1999). For the record or off the record: Comments about the incorporation of Schengen into the EU. *European Journal of Migration and Law, 1*(4), 397–418.

Elsen, C. (2011). Le rôle des accords de Schengen dans la construction européenne. *ERA Forum, 12*(Suppl 1), 69.

Filliez, F., Martenczuk, B., & Van Thiel, S. (2008). Schengen/Dublin: The association agreements with Iceland, Norway, and Switzerland. In *Justice, liberty, security: New challenges for EU external relations* (pp. 145–183).

Golenvaux, P. (1994). La libre circulation des personnes. In Balthazar et al. (Eds.), *Regards sur le Benelux* (Vol. 50, p. 331).

Huybreghts, G. (2015). The Schengen Convention and the Schengen Acquis: 25 years of evolution. *Era Forum, 16*(3), 379–426.

References

Martenczuk, B. (2008). Variable geometry and the external relations of the European Union: The experience of justice and home affairs. In *Justice, liberty, security: New challenges for EU external relations* (pp. 493–525). VUBPRESS.

Papagianni, G. (2006). *Institutional and policy dynamics of EU migration law*. Brill.

Peers, S. (1999). Caveat Emptor? Integrating the Schengen Acquis into the European Union legal order. *Cambridge Yearbook of European Legal Studies, 2*, 87–123.

Peers, S. (2016). *EU justice and home affairs law* (Vol. 1). Oxford University Press.

Picarra, N. (1998). La mise en oeuvre du protocol integrant l'acquis de Schengen dans le cadre de l'Union europèenne: règles et procédures. *Schengen's Final Days*.

Schieffer, M. (2008). Readmission and repatriation of illegal residents. In B. Martenczuk & S. van Thiel (Eds.), *Justice, liberty and security: New challenges for EU external relations*.

Schutte, J. J. (1991). Schengen: Its meaning for the free movement of persons in Europe. *Common Market Law Review, 28*, 549.

Taschner, H. C. (1997). *Schengen: die Übereinkommen zum Abbau der Personenkontrollen an den Binnengrenzen von EU-Staaten*. Nomos-Verlag-Ges.

Turack, D. C. (1968). Freedom of movement and the travel document in Benelux. *International & Comparative Law Quarterly, 17*(1), 191–206.

Wichmann, N. (2006). The participation of the Schengen associates: Inside or outside? *European Foreign Affairs Review, 11*(1), 87.

Zaiotti, R. (2011). *Cultures of border control: Schengen and the evolution of European frontiers*. University of Chicago Press.

Chapter 3
Scope of Schengen Acquis in 2024

There is currently (in May 2024) no updated and authentic EU repository of the Schengen acquis. Each Schengen act is labelled as such in its recitals and can therefore be retrieved and identified in the Official Journal and via the European Union EUR-Lex website. The latest official overviews of the evolving Schengen acquis were published in the annexes of the 2008 EU-Switzerland Schengen Association agreement (OJ L 53, 27.2.2008, pp. 52–79) and the 2011 Liechtenstein Schengen Association Protocol (OJ L 160, 18.6.2011, pp. 3–18). Moreover, Annex II to the 2012 Act of Accession of Croatia (OJ L 112, 24.4.2012, pp. 21–93) listed those provisions of the Schengen acquis which are binding and applicable from the date of accession. Next to that, the governments of Denmark and of Schengen Associated States make available, on their official websites, consolidated overviews. See, for instance, the list provided by the Danish Ministry of Justice at: Oversigt over vedtagne retsakter, der er omfattet af Danmarks retsforbeh....pdf (justitsministeriet.dk) and a reader friendly overview at the Swiss Fedlex website: https://www.fedlex.admin.ch/de/sector-specific-agreements/EU-acts-register/8/8.4 (both accessed in May 2024).

The substantive scope of the Schengen acquis, as it presents itself in 2024, is not as clear and coherent as it should be from the perspective of legal certainty. As explained above in Sects. 2.4–2.6, this status quo is the consequence of historical developments and political decisions taken over the last decades, in the context of which legal and logical arguments were sometimes superseded by political considerations. The Schengen acquis, as it presents itself in 2024, can best be illustrated by the picture of an onion:

© The Author(s), under exclusive license to Springer Nature Switzerland AG 2024
F. Lutz, *Practical Guide to Schengen Law*, SpringerBriefs in Law, https://doi.org/10.1007/978-3-031-56898-5_3

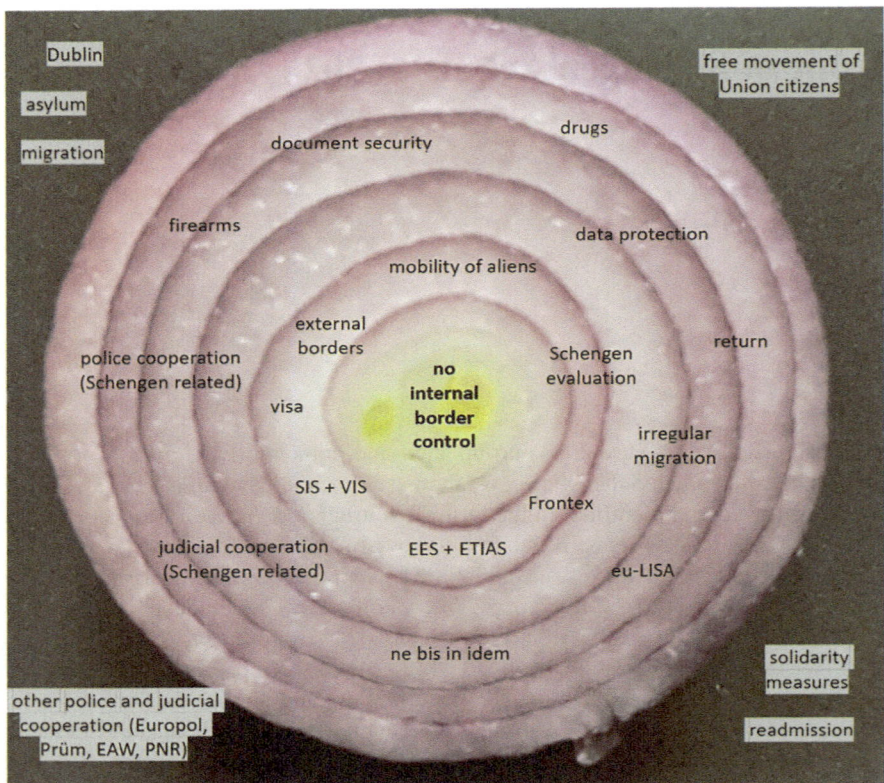

3.1 The Inner Layers

The inner layers of that onion are uncontested and "pure" Schengen acquis. Legal developments in these fields have always and consistently been labelled as Schengen-related.

3.1.1 Abolishment of Internal Border Control

The heart of the Schengen acquis, undoubtedly, consists of the rules providing for the abolishment of internal border control, together with provisions on the possible temporary reintroduction of border control in exceptional circumstances and possibilities for the exercise of police powers and checks in border areas. Already the title of the 1985 Schengen Agreement ("Agreement on the gradual abolition of checks at common borders") shows that its principal objective was the abolition of

3.1 The Inner Layers
39

checks on persons at the common borders of the Member States. These rules were then transformed into legally binding provisions and included, at a prominent place, in Article 2 of the 1990 Convention Implementing the Schengen Agreement. Today they can be found, after the integration of the Schengen acquis into the framework of the European Union in 1999, and after their transformation into an EU regulation, in Articles 25–35 of the Schengen Borders Code Regulation (EU) 2016/399. A proposal (COM(2021)891) for an overhaul of these provisions was adopted by the EU legislature in May 2024. The fact that the abolition of internal border controls constitutes the heart of Schengen was also expressly confirmed by the European Court of Justice in paragraph 83 of its judgment in case C-77/05, *United Kingdom/Council*, where the Court stated: "It should be recalled that both the title of the Schengen Agreement and the fourth recital in its preamble and Article 17 of the agreement show that its principal objective was the abolition of checks on persons at the common borders of the Member States and the transfer of those checks to their external borders."

When was internal border control abolished, and between which States?
Internal border control was abolished in 1995 between a first group of seven Schengen States (the five signatories: Belgium, Germany, France, Luxembourg, Netherlands plus Spain and Portugal which had joined in 1991). Controls to Italy and Austria were lifted in 1998; to Greece in 2000; to Denmark, Sweden, Finland, Norway and Iceland in 2001; to Poland, Czech Republic, Slovakia, Hungary, Slovenia, Lithuania, Latvia, Estonia and Malta in 2007; to Switzerland in 2008; to Liechtenstein in 2011; to Croatia in 2023 and to Romania and Bulgaria in 2024 (for air and sea borders, but not yet for land borders). Internal border control to Cyprus was not lifted yet.

Where can I find a list of notifications of temporary reintroductions of border control at internal borders?
A complete list of Member States' notifications of the temporary reintroduction of border control at internal borders pursuant to Article 25 and 28 et seq. of the Schengen Borders Code is available at the Commissions home affairs website: https://home-affairs.ec.europa.eu/policies/schengen-borders-and-visa/schengen-area/temporary-reintroduction-border-control_en (accessed in May 2024).

> **What is the difference between internal border control and (authorised) exercise of police powers and checks in border areas?**
> In accordance with Schengen rules, the absence of border controls at internal borders does not affect the exercise of police powers by competent authorities of the Member States under national law, insofar as the exercise of those powers does not have an effect equivalent to border checks. The exact delimitation of (authorised) exercise of police powers and checks in border areas was already subject of several European Court of Justice judgements (judgements in cases C-188/10 *Melki*; C-278/12 *Adil*; C-444/17 *Arib*). In 2017, the European Commission issued (Recommendation (EU) 2017/820) on proportionate police checks and police cooperation in the Schengen area in which it provided a non-exhaustive list of measures which could be legitimately taken by Member State authorities in border areas and which, in the Commission view, would not have an effect equivalent to border checks.

3.1.2 Harmonized Rules on External Borders and Visa

The heart of Schengen (abolition of internal border control as set out above in Sect. 3.1.1) is surrounded by a first layer of directly related essential measures: Harmonized rules on the crossing of external borders including harmonized entry conditions for short stays (previously regulated in Articles 3–8 of the Convention Implementing the Schengen Agreement and now set out in title II of the Schengen Borders Code Regulation (EU) 2016/399) and in the new Screening Regulation (EU) 2024/1356) as well as harmonized rules for short-stay visa (previously regulated in Articles 9–17 of the Convention Implementing the Schengen Agreement and now set out in the Visa Code Regulation (EC) No 810/2009 and the Visa List Regulation (EU) 2018/1806). Rules for long-stay visa remain covered by national law and/or EU migration law, but Article 18 of the Convention Implementing the Schengen Agreement (in conjunction with Article 21(2)(a) of the Convention Implementing the Schengen Agreement) grants these "D-visa" Schengen wide effect for short-term stays in other Schengen States. These rules are accompanied by related legal instruments, addressing specific border and visa aspects, such as Regulation (EC) No 1931/2006 laying down rules on local border traffic and Regulations 693/2003/EC and 694/2003/EC on a specific Facilitated Transit Document (FTD) and a Facilitated Rail Transit Document (FRTD).

The Frontex Agency (Regulation (EU) 2019/1896 on the European Border and Coast Guard) assists Member States with implementing the operational aspects of external border management and return. It is complemented by Regulation (EU) No 656/2014 establishing rules for the surveillance of the external sea borders in the context of operational cooperation coordinated by Frontex.

The delimitation between the rules on short stays of third-country nationals, which are fully harmonized by the Schengen acquis (Schengen rules on visa and

Schengen rules on visa-free short-term stay), and the rules on long stays of third-country nationals (rules on issuing residence permits and long-stay visa), which are covered by "normal" EU law and national law, sometimes pose tricky legal questions.

What are the criteria for distinguishing short- and long-term stay?
The relevant criterion for distinguishing short- and long-term stay is the *intended* length of overall stay in the Schengen area, when entering the Schengen area. If the intended overall period of stay is less than 90 days (such as in the case of tourists and business visitors), then the stay is considered as short-term stay and a short stay visa (Schengen visa) may be required upon entry. If the intended overall period of stay is more than 90 days (such as in the case of third-country students, third-country researchers, third-country nationals arriving for family reunification purposes or for seeking international protection) than the stay is considered as long-term stay and a long-stay visa (national "D"-visa) may be required upon entry. This was expressly confirmed by the European Court of Justice in its judgement in case C 638/16, *X and X*: "*An application for a visa ..., on the basis of Article 25 of the Visa code, ..., with a view to lodging, immediately upon his or her arrival in that Member State, an application for international protection and, thereafter, to staying in that Member State for more than 90 days in a 180-day period, does not fall within the scope of that code but, as European Union law currently stands, solely within that of national law.*"

How, exactly, is the length of a short stay calculated?
The wording originally used in the Convention Implementing the Schengen Agreement for describing a short stay ("*three months during the six months following the date of first entry*") posed problems and allowed for differing calculation methods. Pursuant to Case C-241/05 *Bot*, in the context of which these calculation problems became visible, the Union legislator decided to amend, by means of Regulation (EU) No 610/2013, the rules dealing with the calculation of the authorized length of short-term stays in the Union and to provide for mathematically precise, clear, and harmonized rules in all legal acts dealing with this issue (Convention Implementing the Schengen Agreement, Schengen Borders Code, Visa Format Regulation, Visa List Regulation, VIS Regulation, and Visa Code Regulation). These new rules now apply, in the same way, both to visa free and visa obliged short stays. A "Schengen calculator" was developed as a practical tool for travellers. This calculator is available at the Commissions home affairs website: https://home-affairs.ec.europa.eu/policies/schengen-borders-and-visa/border-crossing/short-stay-visa-calculator_en (accessed in May 2024). The Entry/Exit System Regulation provides, in its Article 11, for an express legal basis for an automated calculator to be included in the Entry-Exit System (EES).

Can there be a short stay exceeding 90 days?
Article 20(2) of the Convention Implementing the Schengen Agreement allows the exceptional *extension* of a short-term stay beyond 90 days, in a purely national context, based on existing bilateral agreements. Article 60 of the Entry-Exit System (EES) Regulation (EU) 2017/2226 added subparagraphs 2(a)–2(d) to the text of Article 20 of the Convention Implementing the Schengen Agreement and included specific rules how such extension may be entered in the Entry/Exit System. These provisions will become applicable with start of operation of the Entry-Exit System (EES).

Where can a find a list of the bilateral agreements allowing for an extension of a short stay beyond 90 days?
A list of Member States' bilateral visa waiver agreements with third countries allowing for an extension of the period of stay in accordance with Article 20(2), point (b), of the Convention implementing the Schengen Agreement was published in the Official Journal C 130 of 8.4.2019 on p. 17. This list can also be acceded at EUR-lex under the reference 52019XC0408(02).

Should the 90 days of general 'Schengen' visa-free stay be deducted from the period of visa-free stay provided for by the bilateral agreements?
Interestingly, the long-established understanding by the Commission and Member States is that the duration of stay under an existing bilateral agreement may be *added* to the duration of stay under Schengen rules and that there is no need to deduct the 90 days that are authorised anyhow under general Schengen rules from the period of stay granted by the bilateral agreements. This has been explained, for instance, in the 2014 proposal for the touring visa (COM(2014)163): "… *the provisions of that bilateral agreement may serve as a basis for that Member State to 'extend' a visa-free stay for longer than three months in its territory for nationals of the third country concerned. Thus, for example, citizens of Canada, New Zealand or the United States can stay in such Member States for the period provided by the bilateral visa waiver agreement in force between the Member States and these three countries (usually three months), in addition to the general 90-day stay in the Schengen area.*"

Is it possible to combine a long-term stay with a short stay (after the long-term stay) without leaving?

A third-country national may start a short stay directly after a long-term stay (based on a residence permit or a long-stay visa) without being obliged to leave the EU in between. This was clarified and illustrated with practical examples on pages 40–41 of the 2022 revision of the "Practical Handbook for Border Guards" (Annex to Commission Recommendation C(2022)7591 of 28 October 2022).

Why are the conditions of long-term stay not regulated by Schengen rules?

There are historical but no logical explanation for this fact: One can easily make the case that harmonization of legal migration and asylum rules should also have been considered as necessary flanking measures for the abolition of internal border control and in its judgment in case Wijsenbeek (C-378/97), the European Court of Justice even spelled out that the abolishment of internal border control presupposes harmonisation of the laws of the Member States governing the crossing of the external borders of the Community, *immigration*, the grant of visas, *asylum*, and the exchange of information on those questions. It emerged from research interviews (Chap. 5 of this Guide) that the historical reason for the non-inclusion of long-term stay in the scope of Schengen was, that the policy field of asylum and legal migration was, in general, considered by the five signatories of the Schengen Agreements as too "complicated and heavy" for including it in the Convention Implementing the Schengen Agreement.

3.1.3 Harmonized Rules on Mobility of Legally Staying Third-Country Nationals

Abolition of internal border checks cannot be selective and apply only to EU citizens, since it is impossible—in the absence of checks—to distinguish EU citizens from third-country nationals. Therefore, harmonized conditions governing the intra-Schengen movement of legally staying third-country nationals were set out, as a key flanking measure, in the still directly applicable Articles 19–22 of the Convention Implementing the Schengen Agreement (as amended by Regulations (EU) 265/2010 and 610/2013) distinguishing between the right to Schengen mobility of holders of uniform visa (Article 19 of the Convention Implementing the Schengen Agreement), the right to Schengen mobility of visa free third-country nationals on a short-term stay (Article 20 of the Convention Implementing the Schengen Agreement) and the right to Schengen mobility of third-country holders of residence permits/long-stay visa (Article 21 of the Convention Implementing the Schengen Agreement). A general reporting obligation for third-country nationals is provided for in Article 22 of the Convention Implementing the Schengen Agreement, that was changed from a "shall" to a "may" clause in 2013.

> **Where can I find a list of all types of valid residence permits?**
> A list of those residence permits which have been notified to the Commission in accordance with the obligation under Article 39(1)(a) Schengen Borders Code can be found in Annex 22 to the Practical Handbook for Border Guards (C(2022) 7591 final). A copy of annex 22 is available at the European Commissions home affairs website under the following link: https://home-affairs.ec.europa.eu/system/files/2024-01/handbook-annex-22_en.pdf (accessed in May 2024).

> **Which Member States provide for a reporting obligation under Article 22 of the Convention Implementing the Schengen Agreement?**
> The reporting obligation under Article 22 of the Convention Implementing the Schengen Agreement is also referred to in Article 23(d) of the Schengen Borders Code, as a measure not affected by the absence of border control at internal borders. In accordance with Article 42 Schengen Borders Code, Member States which provide for a reporting obligation need to notify the Commission thereof and this information shall be published in the C Series of the Official Journal. See: Initial notifications by 27 Schengen States (OJ C 18, 24.1.2008, p. 25); Notification by Italy, Slovakia, and update by Malta (OJ C 207, 14.8.2008, p. 10); Notification by Switzerland (OJ C 50, 3.3.2009, p. 10); Notification by Slovenia (OJ C 53, 25.2.2014, p. 27); Notification by Romania (OJ C 417, 16.11.2018, p. 28). A list, with hyperlinks to the publications in the Official Journal, is available at the European Commissions home affairs website under the following link: https://home-affairs.ec.europa.eu/system/files/2020-09/notifications_article_42.pdf (accessed in May 2024).

The "Schengen mobility" of legally staying third-country nationals under Articles 19–22 of the Convention Implementing the Schengen Agreement differs significantly and provides fewer rights than the right to free movement of Union citizens. Schengen mobility of legally staying third-country nationals is limited to

3.1 The Inner Layers

short stays of a maximum of 90 days in other Member States, it depends on the continued fulfilment of the entry conditions set out in Article 6(1) Schengen Borders Code and it does not confer a right to work in other Member States. The "Schengen mobility" under the Convention Implementing the Schengen Agreement must also not be confused with the provisions on intra-EU mobility of legally residing third-country nationals, contained in the EUs legal migration directives. The latter go beyond and complement the mere "Schengen mobility" and can be found in the Long-Term Residents Directive 2003/109/EC, the Blue Card Directive (EU) 2021/1883, the ICT Directive 2014/66/EU as well as in the Students and Researchers Directive (EU) 2016/801.

It is also important to bear in mind that the Schengen acquis only refers to the legality of stay of third-country nationals and not to their right to work. The exercise of economic activities by third-country nationals is an issue which is covered by "normal" EU law as well as national law. It may, however, impact the application of Schengen rules.

Do Schengen rules regulate the right to work during short stays in the EU?
No. Schengen rules only deal with the legality of stay of third-country nationals. Access to the labour market is outside—*ratione materiae*—the scope of the Schengen acquis. A third-country national who is legally staying in a Schengen State, based on a short stay visa or visa free, has no right to work there under Schengen rules. He/she may, however, be allowed to exercise certain forms of economic activities under national or international law.

Is it relevant, from a Schengen law perspective, whether a third-country national on short term stay in EU is working or not?
Yes, it is. Article 6(3) of the Visa List Regulation (EU) 2018/1806 provides that Member States may provide for exceptions from visa free status for persons carrying out a paid activity during their stay. According to the Commissions Visa Handbook (C(2020)395 of 28.1.2020, p. 12), this exception to the exemption from the visa requirement in Article 6(3) should, however, be interpreted narrowly: "*In particular, it should not concern persons employed or exercising an independent activity in their country of residence who have to travel for professional purposes. In that sense, and in accordance with the Visa Waiver Agreements concluded by the EU with certain third countries, this exception should not cover: business persons, i.e. persons travelling for business purposes (without being employed in the Member State of destination); sports persons and artists performing an activity on an ad hoc basis; journalists sent by the media of their country of residence; and*

> *intra-corporate trainees."* A list of the national derogations from the visa requirement, including national requirements under Article 6(3) of the Visa List Regulation (EU) 2018/1806 are publicly available at the Commissions Justice and Home Affairs website: https://home-affairs.ec.europa.eu/policies/schengen-borders-and-visa/visa-policy/who-must-apply-schengen-visa_en (accessed in May 2024).

3.1.4 Large-Scale Schengen IT Systems

Another key component of Schengen are its large scale information systems, which are necessary to implement and police the harmonized Schengen rules: The Schengen Information System, previously regulated in Articles 92–119 of the Convention Implementing the Schengen Agreement, and today composed of Regulations (EU) 2018/1860 (SIS-return), 2018/1861 (SIS-borders) and 2018/1862 (SIS police/judicial cooperation); the Visa Information System (VIS Regulation (EC) No 767/2008); the Entry Exit System (Regulation (EU) 2017/2226); the European Travel Information and Authorization System (ETIAS) (Regulation (EU) 2018/1240); and the framework for interoperability between EU information systems in the field of borders and visa (Regulation (EU) 2019/817).

3.1.5 Schengen Evaluation System

Still close to the core of the Schengen acquis is the Schengen-specific peer review mechanism, which had been originally created by a 1998 Executive Committee Decision setting up Schengen Evaluation (SCH/Com-ex (98)26 def)). Today, the legal frame for Schengen Evaluation is set up by Regulation (EU) 2022/922 of 9 June 2022 on the establishment and operation of an evaluation and monitoring mechanism to verify the application of the Schengen acquis. The legal basis for that Schengen Evaluation Regulation is Article 70 TFEU. That Treaty article provides for the application of a special legislative procedure (Council acting on a proposal of the Commission, without involvement of the European Parliament as co-decision maker). The fact that the ordinary legislative procedure is not applicable in this field, is a heritage of the intergovernmental past of Schengen.

What is the scope of application of the Schengen Evaluation Mechanism?

Article 2(1) of the Schengen Evaluation Regulation (EU) 2022/922 defines the term "Schengen acquis" as: *the provisions integrated into the framework of the Union in accordance with Protocol No 19 on the Schengen acquis integrated into the framework of the European Union, annexed to the TEU and the TFEU, together with the acts building upon them or otherwise related to them.* The last element of this definition ("acts otherwise related") provides interpretative leeway for broadening the scope of the Schengen Evaluation Mechanism beyond the scope of the legal acts which are formally labelled as Schengen-related in their recitals and to also include some of the "lost children of Schengen", mentioned in Sects. 2.4.3 and 2.6.4 of this guide, as well as possibly also the "aura" of the Schengen acquis, as referred to in Sect. 3.3 of this guide. The currently applied scope of application of Schengen Evaluation is reflected in the annual evaluation programmes, covering primarily external borders, return, visa policy, the Schengen Information System (SIS), data protection and police cooperation, the correct application of which are important for a good functioning of the Schengen area. These evaluation programs are adopted in the form of Commission Implementing Decisions (see, for instance, the evaluation programme 2023, adopted on 13.1.2023 under the reference C(2023)56).

What is a "Schengen Catalogue"?

Schengen catalogues are Council Documents, containing recommendations and best practices of implementation of Schengen rules, covering, for instance, the field of external borders and return (Council document 7864/09) and the field of police cooperation (Council Document 15785/2/10 REV 2). Due to their nature (simple Council documents), the Schengen Catalogues are legally non binding "soft-law" documents. Article 14(2) of the Schengen Evaluation Regulation (EU) 2022/922 refers to Schengen catalogues as source of input for the standard questionnaire to be adopted under Article 14 of the Schengen Evaluation Regulation. The Schengen catalogues are publicly accessible, under the above-mentioned references at the Council website.

What is a Handbook?

Handbooks are soft law instruments, containing guidelines, best practices and recommendations, with the aim of ensuring a harmonised application of binding legal provisions. Handbooks are adopted/published in various legal forms, such as Commission recommendations, Commission implementing decisions or Council documents. The use of handbooks is a frequent practice to foster harmonised application of Union law and it is not limited to the field of Schengen acquis. Normally, handbooks are based on advance consultation, discussion and consensus with relevant national experts and therefore enjoy high practical relevance.

Article 14(2) of the Schengen Evaluation Regulation (EU) 2022/922 refers to handbooks as source of input for the standard questionnaire to be adopted under Article 14 of the Schengen Evaluation Regulation. The most relevant handbooks in the field of Schengen are:

The Practical Handbook for Border Guards (Schengen Handbook) (Commission Recommendation C(2022)7591);

The Visa Code Handbook (Commission Implementing Decision C(2020)395);

The Schengen Information System (SIS) Handbook C(2023)2152, as well as the SIRENE Manual—Borders and return C(2021)7900 and the SIRENE Manual—Police C(2021)7901;

The Return Handbook (Commission Recommendation (EU) 2017/2338);

The Manual on cross-border (police) operations (Council document 13887/20 and 13920/20).

3.2 The Outer Layers

The outer layers of the Schengen acquis are still closely related to Schengen and contain a number of provisions which are clearly considered as Schengen-related. The Schengen labelling in these layers happened, however, in a less consistent way than in the inner layers, and legal debates on Schengen-relatedness emerged. In many cases, Schengen-related acts and non-Schengen-related acts coexist side by side, even though they cover closely related substance matters. The below enumeration follows the sequence provided by 1990 Convention Implementing the Schengen Agreement and not the degree of Schengen-relatedness as seen from today's perspective. An informal consolidated version of Convention Implementing the Schengen Agreement can be found in the annex to this guide. It is recommended to use that annex as a complementary tool for understanding the very complex legal situation in the outer layers of Schengen, described in this section.

3.2.1 Document Security

The validity and recognition of documents which demonstrate the identity of persons and their right to cross borders had already been present, as cross cutting issue, in numerous provisions of the Convention Implementing the Schengen Agreement

3.2 The Outer Layers

(Articles 2, 5, 6, 13, 14 and 17). Todays common standards in relation to document security are still mainly Schengen-related. They are laid down in: Regulation (EC) No 2252/2004 on standards for security features and biometrics in passports and travel documents issued by Member States (labelled as pure Schengen instrument); Regulation (EC) No 1030/2002 laying down a uniform format for residence permits for third-country nationals (labelled as hybrid instrument); Regulation (EC) No 1683/95 laying down a uniform format for visas (until 2008 labelled as hybrid instrument, since 2013 labelled as pure Schengen instrument); and Regulation (EC) No 333/2002 on a uniform format for forms for affixing the visa issued by Member States to persons holding travel documents not recognized by the Member State drawing up the form (labelled as hybrid instrument). Third-country travel documents are addressed by Decision No 1105/2011/EU on the list of travel documents which entitle the holder to cross the external borders, and which may be endorsed with a visa and on setting up a mechanism for establishing this list (labelled as pure Schengen instrument). The only Regulation in this field that is not labelled as Schengen-related, due to its close link to free movement rules, is Regulation (EU) 2019/1157 on strengthening the security of identity cards of Union citizens and of residence documents issued to Union citizens and their family members exercising their right of free movement. Interestingly, the European Court of Justice found in its judgment in case C-61/22 that by adopting Regulation 2019/1157 on the basis of Article 21(2) TFEU, the EU legislature infringed Article 77(3) TFEU and had recourse to an inappropriate legislative procedure. It remains to be seen whether the new regulation that will have to be proposed to replace it will be labelled as a Schengen act.

> **Where can I find lists of valid third-country travel documents?**
> Article 9 of Decision 1105/2011/EU provides that the Commission shall make available to the Member States and the public the list of recognized third-country travel documents as well as a list of known fantasy and camouflage passports via a constantly updated electronic publication. A reader-friendly and structured overview of the available lists (Travel documents issued by third countries and territorial entities; Travel documents issued by Member States and Schengen Associated States; Travel documents issued by international organisations and other entities subject to international law; List of fantasy and camouflage passports) with hyperlinks is available at https://www.consilium.europa.eu/prado/en/prado-recognised-documents.html (accessed in May 2024).

3.2.2 Return and Readmission

Both return and readmission had originally constituted a part of the Schengen acquis. Council decided, however, from 2000 onwards, to consider readmission as a non-Schengen-related matter (see above Sect. 2.9.2). Contrary to readmission, the field of return of illegally staying third-country nationals kept its Schengen nature. It had been covered by Articles 23 and 24 of the Convention Implementing the Schengen Agreement, which were replaced, in 2008, by the Return Directive (EC) 2008/115. The Return Directive was formally labelled as "hybrid instrument," i.e., constituting both part of the Schengen acquis and part of the "normal" irregular migration acquis. Specific aspects of return are also addressed by Directive 2001/40/EC on the mutual recognition of decisions on the expulsion of third-country nationals (labelled as hybrid instrument), Directive 2003/110/EC on assistance in cases of transit for the purposes of removal by air (labelled as hybrid instrument), Council Decision 2004/573/EC on the organization of joint flights for removals from the territory of two or more Member States, of third-country nationals who are subjects of individual removal orders (labelled as hybrid instrument). and the new Return Border Regulation (EU) 2024/1349 (proposed by the Commission in COM(2020)611 as linked to asylum procedures and therefore not Schengenrelated, but adopted by EP and Council as self-standing "pure" Schengen instrument).

3.2.3 Irregular Migration

As regards the fight against irregular migration, Article 26 of the Convention Implementing the Schengen Agreement contains provisions on carriers' liability, which are still in force, supplemented by Directive 2001/51/EC (labelled as hybrid instrument). The Advance Passenger Information (API) Directive 2004/82/EC (labelled as pure Schengen instrument) provides obligations on carriers to communicate passenger data. That Directive will be replaced, in autumn 2024, by a new Schengen API-Border Regulation (next to a non-Schengen API-Law Enforcement Regulation) Framework Decision 2002/946/JHA (labelled as pure Schengen instrument) and Directive 2002/90/EC (labelled as hybrid instrument) address the facilitation of unauthorized entry, transit, and residence. There is also Regulation (EU) 2019/1240 on the creation of a European network of immigration liaison officers (recast) (labelled as pure Schengen instrument). Other measures addressing the challenge of irregular migration were adopted as non-Schengen-related acts, such as Directive 2011/36/EU on preventing and combatting trafficking in human beings and protecting its victims and the Employers Sanctions Directive 2009/52/EC.

3.2.4 Police Cooperation

The Schengen-related aspects of police cooperation were created by the Convention Implementing the Schengen Agreement and remain, until today, primarily based on a direct application of its Articles 39–47:

- Articles 39 and 46 of the Convention Implementing the Schengen Agreement contain rules on information exchange between police authorities, which were further developed and partly replaced by Framework Decision 2006/960/JHA on simplifying the exchange of information and intelligence between law enforcement authorities of the Member States of the European Union ("Swedish Initiative"—labelled as Schengen related). From 12 December 2024, the parts of

3.2 The Outer Layers

Articles 39 and 46 that have not been replaced by Framework Decision 2006/960/JHA are replaced by Directive (EU) 2023/977 on the exchange of information between the law enforcement authorities of Member States and repealing Council Framework Decision 2006/960/JHA, in so far as those Articles relate to the exchange of information falling within the scope of that Directive. Articles 39 and 46 continue to be applicable to other forms of police cooperation falling outside the scope of that Directive

- Article 40 of the Convention Implementing the Schengen Agreement (amended by Council Decision 2003/725/JHA amending the provisions of Article 40(1) and (7) of the Convention Implementing the Schengen Agreement) provides for common rules on cross-border surveillance.
- Article 41 of the Convention Implementing the Schengen Agreement regulates the conditions of hot pursuit in the territory of other Schengen States.
- Articles 42 and 43 of the Convention Implementing the Schengen Agreement regulate the position and liabilities of officers who are conducting cross border surveillance and hot pursuit.
- Articles 44 and 47 of the Convention Implementing the Schengen Agreement provide for tools for information exchange, including law enforcement liaison officers. The latter aspect was further developed by Council Decision 2003/170/JHA on the common use of liaison officers posted abroad by the law enforcement agencies of the Member States (labelled as Schengen-related).
- Finally, Article 45 provides for a far-reaching obligation on those offering hotel or other accommodation to require all foreigners (both third-country nationals and nationals of other Member States) to confirm their identity and to sign registration forms.

The above-mentioned Schengen-related police cooperation measures coexist with numerous other non-Schengen-related police cooperation measures which have been adopted at EU level as "normal" EU law, such as: The Prüm II Framework (Decisions 2008/615/JHA and 2008/616/JHA); the European Union Agency for Law Enforcement Cooperation (Europol) (Regulation (EU) No 2016/794); the European Union Agency for Law Enforcement Training (CEPOL) (Regulation (EU) 2015/2219); the Passenger Name Record (PNR) Directive (EU) 2016/681; the Data Retention Directive 2006/24/EC (declared invalid in 2014); Directive (EU) 2019/1153 facilitating the use of financial and other information for the prevention, detection, investigation or prosecution of certain criminal offences and Regulation (EU) 2019/818 on establishing a framework for interoperability between EU information systems in the field of police and judicial cooperation, asylum and migration (hybrid instrument). The Schengen Associated States participate in some of these non-Schengen-related police cooperation measures on the basis of separately concluded international agreements, such as the 2019 Agreement between the EU and Switzerland and the 2008 Agreement with Norway and Iceland on the application of certain provisions of the Prüm Decisions, and bilateral operational agreements concluded between Europol and Norway (2001), Iceland (2001), Switzerland (2004) and Liechtenstein (2013).

Looking at the substance of the police cooperation issues addressed, it is difficult to understand the separation between Schengen-related and non-Schengen-related forms of police cooperation. As explained above in Sect. 2.6 of this guide, the currently existing separation can only be explained by political reasons which steered the relevant decisions made by the legislator.

3.2.5 Mutual Assistance in Criminal Matters

Mutual assistance in criminal matters is addressed by Articles 48–53 of the Convention Implementing the Schengen Agreement. These Schengen provisions built upon and supplemented/widened the provisions of the 1959 (Council of Europe) European Convention on Mutual Assistance in Criminal Matters, which required States to afford each other the widest measure of mutual assistance in proceedings in respect of offences the punishment of which falls within the jurisdiction of the judicial authorities of the requesting Party. The provisions of the Convention Implementing the Schengen Agreement were further developed by Council Act of 29 May 2000 establishing the Convention on Mutual Assistance in Criminal Matters between the Member States of the European Union (a sui generis hybrid legal instrument—see its article 2).

The subsequently adopted Framework Decision 2008/978/JHA on the European Evidence Warrant (EEW) as well as Directive 2014/41/EU regarding the European Investigation Order in criminal matters were labelled as non-Schengen-related JHA instruments. The latter left, however, unaffected (see Article 34 of Directive 2014/41EU) the possibility for Member States to apply pre-existing instruments (such as the 2000 Council Convention on Mutual Assistance in Criminal Matters and the Convention Implementing the Schengen Agreement) in their relations with third countries (i.e. Norway, Iceland, Switzerland and Liechtenstein) as well as in their relations with other Member States not bound by Directive 2014/41/EU (Denmark and Ireland). This approach implied that some Articles of the Convention Implementing the Schengen Agreement still remain in force for Schengen Associated States, while they were repealed for other States (Huybreghts, 2015, p. 391). It also implied that in this policy field two sets of rules co-exist: the "frozen" Schengen-related judicial co-operation as applied between the Member States at the time of entry into force of the Amsterdam Treaty and the more far-reaching, formally non-Schengen-related EU rules adopted after 1999.

3.2.6 Ne bis in idem

The application of the ne bis in idem principle is regulated in Articles 54–58 of the Convention Implementing the Schengen Agreement. Two attempts to replace these Schengen rules by an EU act were made: a 2001 Greek proposal (Council document 6356/03) and a 2009 Czech/Polish/Slovenian/Slovak/Swedish proposal (Council document 5208/09), but didn't succeed. This subject matter therefore remains, until today, fully within the substantive scope of the Schengen acquis. The ne bis in idem principle is, however, also enshrined in Article 50 of the Charter of Fundamental Rights of the EU, which extends the principle throughout Union territory.

3.2.7 Extradition

Extradition is addressed by Articles 59–65 of the Convention Implementing the Schengen Agreement. These Schengen provisions built upon and supplemented/widened the provisions of the 1957 (Council of Europe) European Convention on Extradition. In addition, in the 1990s, two Conventions dealing with extradition had been agreed upon among Member States and formed part of the Union acquis: the Convention of 10 March 1995 on simplified extradition procedure between the Member States of the European Union ("Simplified Extradition Convention"—still not yet in force) and the Convention of 27 September 1996 relating to extradition between the Member States of the European Union ("Extradition Convention", in force since 5 November 2019, see OJ 2019/C 329/02).

From 2004 onwards, Framework Decision 2002/584/JHA on the European Arrest Warrant (EAW) (labelled as non-Schengen-related) replaced, in relations between Member States, all the previous instruments concerning extradition, including the provisions of Articles 59–65 of the Convention Implementing the Schengen Agreement. As regards relations with Schengen Associated States, Decision 2003/169/JHA determined—ex post—that the entire "Simplified Extradition Convention" as well as Articles 2, 6, 8, 9 and 13 of the "Extradition Convention" constituted developments of the Schengen acquis.

In November 2019, a separate Agreement, concluded already in 2006, on the surrender procedure between the Member States of the European Union and Iceland/Norway entered into force. This situation implies, like in the field of mutual assistance in criminal matters, that in this policy field several sets of rules co-exist and that some Articles of the Convention Implementing the Schengen Agreement still remain in force for some Schengen Associated States, while they were repealed for other States (Huybreghts, 2015, pp. 393–394).

3.2.8 Transfer of Enforcement of Criminal Judgments

The transfer of the enforcement of criminal judgments is addressed by Articles 67–69 of the Convention Implementing the Schengen Agreement. These Articles were replaced—as regards their application between Member States but not as regards their application between Member States and third States i.e. Switzerland, Norway, Iceland and Liechtenstein—by Framework Decision 2008/909/JHA on the application of the principle of mutual recognition to judgments in criminal matters imposing custodial sentences or measures involving deprivation of liberty for the purpose of their enforcement in the European Union (labelled as non-Schengen-related).

3.2.9 Drugs

Narcotic Drugs are addressed by Articles 70–76 of the Convention Implementing the Schengen Agreement. The legislative acts adopted after 1999 in this field were all formally considered as non-Schengen-related (no discussion in Mixed Committee and no Schengen recitals): Framework Decision 2004/757 laying down minimum provisions on the constituent elements of criminal acts and penalties in the field of illicit drug trafficking, the drug precursors Regulations (Regulation (EC) No 111/2005 and Regulation (EC) No 273/2004) as well as other EU measures de facto superseded many of the provisions in Articles 70–76 of the Convention Implementing the Schengen Agreement, but the latter were never formally repealed (with the exception of Article 73, dealing with controlled deliveries, which had been repealed by Article 2 of Council Act of 29 May 2000 establishing the Convention on Mutual Assistance in Criminal Matters). In its judgments in cases C-137/09 and C-663/18 the European Court of Justice still refers to Article 71 of the Convention Implementing the Schengen Agreement as applicable and legally binding Schengen measure. This seems to indicate that currently there are also two sets of rules that apply in parallel in this policy field, namely the provisions of the Convention Implementing the Schengen Agreement, which remain applicable amongst Schengen States, and the more developed EU drugs acquis applicable in the EU context.

3.2.10 Firearms and Ammunition

The Schengen nature of EU rules on firearms and ammunition changed twice in the course of history: Articles 77–91 of the Convention Implementing the Schengen Agreement provided a comprehensive regulatory frame on acquisition, possession and trade of firearms and ammunition which was replaced, already in 1991, by Directive 91/477/EEC on control of the acquisition and possession of weapons. This Directive was not formally considered relevant for the definition of the Schengen acquis in 1999. Nevertheless Directive 91/477/EEC was listed in the Annexes of the Norwegian/Iceland and the Swiss as well as the Liechtenstein agreements. The 2008 amendment of the Firearms Directive (Directive 2008/51/EC) did not contain Schengen recitals and thus had to be considered as non-Schengen-related. However, the 2017 amendment of that Directive (Directive 2017/853/EU) as well as its new codified version of 2021 (Directive 2021/555/EU) contain Schengen recitals confirming its Schengen-relatedness for the Schengen Associated States. Directives 2017/853/EU and 2021/555/EU contain no recitals on Ireland and Denmark. For these two Member States the Directive is applicable as "normal" Union law and not as Schengen acquis, since it is based on harmonisation achieved at EC level already before 1999. It may therefore also be categorised as sui generis "hybrid act".

3.2.11 eu-Lisa

The eu-Lisa Regulation (EU) 2018/1726 on the European Union Agency for the Operational Management of Large-Scale IT Systems in the Area of Freedom, Security and Justice is covering the operation of both Schengen-related and non-Schengen-related legal instruments within one comprehensive legal frame and the only feasible way to do so was by using the legal construction of a hybrid act, containing both Schengen-related and non-Schengen-related components.

3.2.12 Transport and Movement of Goods

Articles 120–125 of the Convention Implementing the Schengen Agreement contained rules on transport and movement of goods, with the objective to facilitate movement of goods at internal borders. These Articles were superseded by internal market and customs union rules adopted at EC level. They were therefore printed in italics when the Convention Implementing the Schengen Agreement was published in the Official Journal L 239 of 22.9.2000, but they were never expressly repealed. From a formal point of view, they seem to fall under the category of obsolete Schengen law, referred to in recital 4(d) of Council Decision 1999/435/EC: "The subject matter of the provision is covered by and therefore superseded by existing European Community or Union legislation or by a legal act adopted by all Member States."

3.2.13 Data Protection

Data protection issues are addressed twice by the Convention Implementing the Schengen Agreement: Articles 102–118 address the protection of personal data in the Schengen Information System (SIS). These provisions have been replaced by the above-mentioned SIS acquis (Regulations (EU) 2018/1860, 2018/1861 and 2018/1862). Articles 126–130 deal with general data protection provisions that relate to the whole of the Schengen acquis. These Articles are formally still in place, but they were de facto superseded by the adoption of more detailed legal instruments covering the field of data protection. Todays EU data protection acquis has a non-Schengen-related as well as a Schengen-related component:

Provisions on data protection *in general*—extending beyond the scope of application of Schengen rules—were harmonized at EC level already in 1995 by Directive 95/46/EC on the protection of individuals with regard to the processing of personal data and on the free movement of such data. Directive 95/46/EC had initially been considered as Schengen related, but it was subsequently, in 1999, incorporated into the EEA acquis. This, from a legal point of view rather questionable, "switch" from Schengen-related to EEA-related was announced and endorsed by a "Statement by the Council and the Commission in respect of Directive 95/46/EC", attached to the Norway/Iceland Schengen Association Agreement (OJ L 176, 10.7.1999, p. 61). In spite of that switch, Directive 95/46/EC was nevertheless listed in Annex B of the Swiss Schengen Association Agreement as a Schengen-related act, to the extent that it had replaced and/or developed corresponding provisions of the Convention Implementing the Schengen Agreement. The General Data Protection Regulation (EU) 2016/679, which repealed and replaced Directive 95/46/EC, was then labelled as EEA related and non-Schengen-related (a detailed reasoning for this, arguably, rather political than legal choice was given by Council Legal Service in Council document 12682/12).

As regards data protection in the field of *police and judicial cooperation*, Framework Decision 2008/977/JHA on the protection of personal data processed in the framework of police and judicial cooperation in criminal matters as well as its successor, Directive (EU) 2016/680 on the protection of natural persons with regard to the processing of personal data by competent authorities for the purposes of the prevention, investigation, detection or prosecution of criminal offences or the execution of criminal penalties, were labelled as Schengen-related.

What is a "hybrid instrument"?
The notion of "hybrid instrument" is used for legal acts which are both Schengen-related and non-Schengen-related (i.e., normal Union law) at the same time. From a purely legal point of view, hybrid instruments should not exist, since each legal act should either be labelled as Schengen-related or not, and the resulting variable geometry constellation should be respected in the decision-making procedure. To satisfy policy objectives (involve the greatest possible number of States; avoid drafting of parallel legal texts; changing perception of Schengen-relatedness of certain policy fields) the legislator nevertheless decided to commit the legal "sin" of adopting hybrid instruments in some cases.

How many hybrid instruments exist?
In the field of return, the Return Directive (EC) 2008/115, Directive 2001/40/EC on the mutual recognition of decisions on the expulsion of third-country nationals, Directive 2003/110/EC on assistance in cases of transit for the purposes of removal by air and Council Decision 2004/573/EC on the organization of joint flights for removals were all labelled, in their recitals, as both Schengen-related and at the same time as open for an opt-in of Ireland and

UK under the UK/Ireland Protocol. In these cases, the political reason for creating hybrid instruments was presumably the wish to allow the UK and Ireland to participate and to avoid, at the same time, the need to draft two separate parallel legal instruments (Lutz, 2010, pp. 32–33).

The same approach was followed in the field of irregular migration, when adopting Directive 2001/51/EC supplementing Article 26 of the Convention Implementing the Schengen Agreement (carriers' liability) and Directive 2002/90/EC on facilitation of unauthorized entry, transit, and reside.

In the field of document security, Regulations (EC) No 1030/2002 and (EC) No 333/2002 were labelled as hybrid instruments; Regulation (EC) No 1683/95 was labelled until 2008 as hybrid instrument and since 2013 as pure Schengen instrument.

The codified Firearms Directive (EU) 2021/555 is labelled as Schengen-related for Schengen Associated States, but it contains no recitals on Ireland and Denmark. For these two Member States the Directive is applicable as "normal" Union law and not as Schengen acquis, since it is based on harmonization achieved at EC level already before 1999. It may therefore be categorized as sui generis hybrid act.

The eu-Lisa Regulation (EU) 2018/1726 and the Interoperability Regulation (police and judicial cooperation, asylum, and migration) (EU) 2019/818 are also labelled as hybrid instruments. In both cases, the legislator aimed at covering both Schengen-related and non-Schengen-related measures within one comprehensive legal frame and the only feasible way to do so, was by means of a hybrid act.

Council Act of 29 May 2000 establishing the Convention on Mutual Assistance in Criminal Matters between the Member States of the European Union splits up (in paras 2 and 3) the provisions of this Convention in Schengen-related and non-Schengen-related and therefore constitutes a sui generis hybrid legal instrument.

3.3 The Aura

A number of subject matters that have a direct political linkage to the establishment and operation of an area without internal border are, from a formal legal perspective, not considered as Schengen-related. They were either never considered as Schengen-related (such as the field of legal migration and substantive asylum law), or they were harmonized at EEC level before the creation of Schengen (such as free movement rules), or they only emerged as a relevant topic for Schengen in recent years (such as solidarity measures or responsibility rules for irregular migrants), or they lost their Schengen-relatedness in the course of history (such as Dublin, readmission and many developments in the field of police and judicial cooperation, as explained above in Sect. 3.2).

3.3.1 Asylum and Immigration

The policy fields of Asylum and Immigration could have objectively been considered as closely linked to the establishment of an area without internal border, but they were, from the outset, not included in the scope of the Schengen acquis. These policy fields were also not included in the Benelux rules which served, as explained above in Sect. 2.3, as a blueprint for Schengen. It emerged from research interviews (Chap. 5) that the policy field of asylum and legal migration was, in general, considered as too "complicated and heavy" for including it in the Convention Implementing the Schengen Agreement, with the noteworthy exception of responsibility rules for asylum seekers (Articles 28–38 of the Convention Implementing the Schengen Agreement), which had been designed in view of the single market logic of determining responsible Member States, and not in view of harmonising substantive asylum law.

Since Schengen border management has an undeniable and very close link to the asylum related provisions applicable at the external borders, it can be expected that the linkage between Schengen and asylum law will continue to be discussed at political level. In its 2021 opinion on the Schengen-relatedness of the proposed Pact on Migration and Asylum, the Council Legal Service raised, for instance, the question as to whether the requirement of having an asylum border procedure in place should be part of the Schengen acquis, as a necessary border management measures, while the substantive rules of such a procedure would be regulated in the asylum legislation (Council document 6357/21, para 33).

3.3.2 Responsibility for Processing Asylum Applications (Dublin and Eurodac)

Articles 28–38 of the Convention Implementing the Schengen Agreement contained rules on responsibility for processing applications for asylum. These provisions were replaced, in 1997, by the provisions of the 1990 Dublin Convention, as set out in the 1994 "Bonn Protocol" (Sch/Com-ex (94)3). These so called "Dublin rules" were not considered part of the Schengen acquis at the moment of Amsterdamisation in 1999. It emerged from research interviews (Chap. 5, question 5) that the labelling of Dublin as non-Schengen-related seemed to have been influenced by a strong UK interest in being part of the mechanism, which explains why the Dublin Convention was negotiated and agreed upon nearly in parallel to the very similar rules of Articles 28–38 of the Convention Implementing the Schengen Agreement. On the other hand, UK also seemed to have exercised its influence to make sure that Dublin was not considered as Schengen-related in the 1999 definition of the Schengen acquis.

The Dublin rules were subsequently replaced by "normal" EC/EU Regulations (Council Regulation (EC) No 343/2003 establishing the criteria and mechanisms for determining the Member State responsible for examining an asylum application lodged in one of the Member States by a third-country national, the 2014 recast

Regulation (EU) No 604/2013) and the new Asylum and Migration Management Regulation (EU) 2024/1351). Together with the so called "Eurodac rules" (Council Regulation (EC) No 2725/2000 concerning the establishment of 'Eurodac' for the comparison of fingerprints for the effective application of the Dublin Convention, the 2013 recast Regulation (EU) No 603/2013 and the new Eurodac Regulation (EU) 2024/1358), these regulations are sometimes referred to as "Dublin/Eurodac" acquis. Due to its close link to the Schengen acquis, participation in the Dublin/Eurodac acquis was made a formal condition for participation of Norway, Iceland, Switzerland and Liechtenstein in the Schengen acquis under their Schengen Association Agreements (Article 7 of the Norway/Iceland Schengen Association Agreement and Article 15(4) of the Swiss Schengen Association Agreement) and implementation of the Schengen Association Agreements has to happen hand in hand with the parallel Dublin/Eurodac Association agreements. This formal linkage between the Dublin and the Schengen acquis through the Schengen Association Agreements made the Dublin/Eurodac acquis a special case of "political" but not "legal" Schengen acquis.

3.3.3 Free Movement Rules

As already explained above in Sect. 2.3.4, the abolition of internal border control presupposed, as business basis, the existence of harmonised rules on the free movement of Union citizens. Such rules already existed, in the form of binding EEC law, at the time when the Schengen Agreements were negotiated, and it was neither necessary nor legally possible to include them in the Schengen acquis. Since free movement rules are the business basis for Schengen, any third country wishing to be associated to Schengen must also accept and apply the EU free movement acquis beforehand, as a precondition for joining Schengen.

3.3.4 Solidarity Measures

From the perspective of 2024, it can be argued that the Schengen rules on the establishment of an area without internal border should also have included solidarity measures, applicable in situations in which one (or some) Member States are confronted with a disproportionate burden in terms of protecting the external borders, returning irregular migrants, or receiving asylum seekers. It emerges from research interviews (Chap. 5), that this gap can only be understood against the historical context of the original five Schengen States having no significant external borders and the fact that the Convention Implementing the Schengen Agreement was still negotiated in times in which migratory pressure at external land borders was not yet a pressing political issue. This fact also explains why the Dublin rules, that can be considered, from todays perspective, as placing an unfair burden on frontline

Member States, were considered as fair and agreed upon 40 years ago by the five Schengen signatories.

The lack of solidarity measures was subsequently addressed by financial instruments, which were labelled as Schengen-related only to the extent that they covered external borders and visa (Regulation (EU) 2021/1148 establishing, as part of the Integrated Border Management Fund, the Instrument for Financial Support for Border Management and Visa Policy). The financial instrument covering return (Regulation (EU) 2021/1147 establishing the Asylum, Migration, and Integration Fund) as well as the financial instrument covering police and judicial cooperation (Regulation (EU) 2021/1149 establishing the Internal Security Fund) were not labelled as Schengen-related (explanations for the latter can be found in Council Legal Service opinion 5250/12).

As regards solidarity measures aimed at taking over persons, the EU measures adopted so far (Relocation Decisions (EU) 2015/1523 and (EU) 2015/1601) were labelled as non-Schengen-related, but the role of Schengen Associated States was taken into consideration by article 11 (in both decisions), which expressly encourages bilateral arrangements between the benefitting States (Greece and Italy) and Iceland, Liechtenstein, Norway, and Switzerland. The solidarity part (IV) of the new Asylum and Migration Management Regulation (EU) 2024/1351 is neither labelled as Schengen-related nor as Dublinrelated.

3.3.5 Responsibility Rules for Irregular Migrants

Whilst the Convention Implementing the Schengen Agreement had provided a comprehensive system of responsibility rules for asylum seekers, it had remained largely silent on the responsibility for irregular migrants, i.e., those who don't have a right to stay in a Member State. Article 23(2) of the Convention Implementing the Schengen Agreement (now replaced by Article 6(2) of the Return Directive 2008/115/EC) only addressed one specific case, namely migrants who are illegally staying in State B, whilst holding a right to legal stay in State A. All other cases remained unregulated. In its 2005 proposal for the Return Directive (COM(2005)391), the Commission had proposed to set up a "Dublin-like" system for irregular migrants, but this idea did not find support in Council and the only trace which this idea left in the text of the Return Directive was its article 6(3), which allows Member States to continue the application of existing bilateral readmission agreements with other Member States (Lutz, 2010, p. 17). The issue re-emerged in the Commissions December 2021 proposal for amending the Schengen Borders Code (COM(2021)891), which was adopted by the EU legislature in May 2024, and which contains a new procedure for transferring irregular migrants apprehended at the internal borders (Article 23a). The idea behind this proposal is to provide Member States with a practical tool to react to irregular secondary migratory flows at internal borders, without having to recur to the "heavy" and intrusive policy tool of reintroducing internal border control, which had been increasingly used by Member States since the migration crisis of 2015 (Salomon & Rijpma, 2023, p. 282).

3.3 The Aura

Which JHA Agencies are labelled as Schengen-related and which aren't?

Labelled as *Schengen-related*: European Border and Coast Guard Agency (FRONTEX).

Labelled as *hybrid (partly Schengen-related, partly non-Schengen-related)*: European Union Agency for the Operational Management of Large-Scale IT Systems in the Area of Freedom, Security and Justice (eu-LISA).

Labelled as *not Schengen-related*: European Union Agency for Asylum (EUAA); European Union Agency for Law Enforcement Cooperation (EUROPOL); European Union Agency for Law Enforcement Training (CEPOL), European Union Agency for Criminal Justice Cooperation (Eurojust), European Monitoring Centre for Drugs and Drug Addiction (EMCDDA), European Union Agency for Fundamental Rights (FRA), European Institute for Gender Equality (EIGE).

Are Denmark, Ireland and the Schengen Associated States involved in the operation of these Agencies?

FRONTEX: *Denmark* participates under its special Schengen arrangement of Article 4 of the Denmark Protocol (see recital 125 of Regulation (EU) 2019/1896); *Ireland* does not take part (see recital 127 of Regulation (EU) 2019/1896), but it may be involved in certain activities defined in Article 70 of Regulation (EU) 2019/1896; *Schengen Associated States* participate fully (see recital 121–124 of Regulation (EU) 2019/1896; administrative details are set out in the 2007 Arrangement between the EC and Iceland/Norway on the modalities of those states' participation (OJ L 188, 20.7.2007, pp. 19–23) and in the 2010 Arrangement between the EC and Switzerland/Liechtenstein on the modalities of the participation by those States (OJ L 243, 16.9.2010, pp. 4–15).

eu-LISA: *Denmark* participates partially (in Schengen, Dublin and Eurodac matters; see recital 51 of Regulation (EU) 2018/1726); *Ireland* initially wasn't allowed to participate (see recital 53 of Regulation (EU) 2018/1726) but it subsequently obtained an authorisation to participate, under Article 4 of the Schengen Protocol, by Council Decision 2019/1749 of 14 October 2019; *Schengen Associated States* participate partially (in Schengen, Dublin and Eurodac matters); see recital 54–56 of Regulation (EU) 2018/1726; further details are set out in the 2019 Arrangement between the EU, and Norway, Iceland, Switzerland and Liechtenstein, on the participation by those states in eu-LISA (OJ L 138, 24.5.2019).

EUAA: *Denmark* doesn't participate but it enjoys special observer status (see recitals 63 and 64 and Article 33 of Regulation (EU) 2021/2303); *Ireland* initially didn't opt in (see recital 62 of Regulation (EU) 2021/2303) but it launched internal procedures for doing so in spring 2023 and became bound by the Regulation in August 2023; *Schengen Associated States* don't participate but enjoy special observer status (See recital 65 and Article 34 of Regulation (EU) 2021/2303; further details are due to be set out in an Arrangement to be concluded between the EU, and Norway, Iceland, Switzerland and Liechtenstein, on the participation by those states in EUAA, foreseen by Article 34(2) of Regulation (EU) 2021/2303).

EUROPOL: *Denmark* doesn't participate (see recital 74 of Regulation (EU) 2016/794) but it cooperates with Europol under the 29 April 2017 bilateral "Agreement on Operational and Strategic Cooperation between the Kingdom of Denmark and Europol"; *Ireland* opted in under the UK/Ireland Protocol and participates (see recital 72 of Regulation (EU) 2016/794); *Schengen Associated States* don't participate, but cooperation with these States takes place under bilateral operational agreements concluded before 1 May 2017 (cut-off date foreseen in Article 25 of Regulation (EU) 2016/794) between Europol and Norway (2001), Iceland (2001), Switzerland (2004) and Liechtenstein (2013).

CEPOL: *Denmark* doesn't participate (see recital 26 of Regulation (EU) 2015/2219); *Ireland* initially didn't opt in (see recital 25 of Regulation (EU) 2015/2219) but did so at a later stage, in July 2016 (see Commission Decision (EU) 2016/2063 of 24 November 2016); *Schengen Associated States* don't participate, but cooperation with these states takes place under bilateral working arrangements concluded between CEPOL and Norway (2022), Iceland (2021), Switzerland (2022) and Liechtenstein (2020).

EUROJUST: *Denmark* doesn't participate (see recital 72 of Regulation (EU) 2018/1727) but it cooperates with EUROJUST under a 2019 bilateral "Agreement on Criminal Justice Cooperation"; *Ireland* initially didn't opt in (see recital 71 of Regulation (EU) 2018/1727) but it did so at a later stage (see Commission Decision (EU) 2019/2006 of 29 November 2019); *Schengen Associated States* don't participate, but cooperation with these states takes place under bilateral working arrangements concluded before 12 December 2019 (cut-off date foreseen in Article 56 of Regulation (EU) 2018/1727) between EUROJUST and Norway (2005), Iceland (2005), Switzerland (2008) and Liechtenstein (2013).

EMCDDA: *Denmark* and *Ireland* participate in Regulation (EC) No 1920/2006 on the European Monitoring Centre for Drugs and Drug Addiction (recast) as "normal" EU Member States. Some *Schengen Associated States* cooperate with EMCCDDA on the basis of Agreements: Cooperation with Norway is regulated by an Agreement between the European Community and Norway on the participation of Norway in the work of the EMCDDA (2000); Cooperation with Switzerland takes place under a Working Arrangement between the European Monitoring Centre for Drugs and Drug Addiction and the Federal Office of Public Health of Switzerland (2017).

FRA: *Denmark* and *Ireland* participate in Regulation (EC) No 168/2007 establishing a European Union Agency for Fundamental Rights as "normal" EU Member States. *Schengen Associated States* are not formally involved in work of FRA, but FRA cooperates, on the basis of a 2017 exchange of letters, with the "EEA and Norway Grants" as a partner in the implementation of EEA and Norway Grants funded projects in selected EU Member States.

EIGE: *Denmark* and *Ireland* participate in Regulation (EC) No 1922/2006 on establishing a European Institute for Gender Equality as "normal" EU Member States. *Schengen Associated States* are currently not formally involved in work of EIGE.

References

Huybreghts, G. (2015). The Schengen Convention and the Schengen Acquis: 25 years of evolution. *Era Forum, 16*(3), 379–426.

Lutz, F. (2010). *The negotiations on the return directive: Comments and materials.*

Salomon, S., & Rijpma, J. (2023). A Europe without internal frontiers: Challenging the reintroduction of border controls in the Schengen area in the light of union citizenship. *German Law Journal, 24*(2), 281–309.

Chapter 4
The Territorial Scope of Schengen

4.1 Context

One of the specific features of the Schengen acquis is its complex territorial scope of application that differs from the scope of application of "normal" Union law: Some Member States (Ireland and Denmark) are not bound by the Schengen acquis in principle but can take part via an authorised partial participation (Ireland) or implement it via international law (Denmark). For new Member States (such as Cyprus) a distinction is made between "being bound" by the Schengen acquis (already at moment of accession) and "fully applying" the Schengen acquis (at a later moment, decided upon unanimously by Council). Moreover, four third countries (Norway, Iceland, Switzerland, and Liechtenstein) are bound by the Schengen acquis and can even participate in internal Schengen decision-shaping via a unique Mixed Committee procedure, defined in their Schengen Association Agreements. Next to this "variable geometry" architecture, there are further special aspects of territorial applicability of the Schengen acquis which deserve clarification, such as the rules applicable to the outermost regions of France, Spain and Portugal, the European Microstates (Andorra, San Marino, Monaco, Vatican), Greenland and the Faeroe Islands, Ceuta and Melilla, foreign military bases, Kaliningrad, Mount Athos, Svalbard, the Aland islands, and Gibraltar. These aspects will be dealt with, one by one, in this chapter.

4.2 The Position of Ireland

The position of Ireland, in relation to the Schengen acquis, can only be understood against the background of the Common Travel Area, a long-standing arrangement between the United Kingdom and Ireland that pre-dated both British and Irish membership of the EU, and which provides for free movement between the United Kingdom and Ireland. For geographic and political reasons, in particular the imperative to avoid border control between the Republic of Ireland and Northern Ireland, maintaining the Common Travel Area has always been key for Ireland and was considered more important than joining the Schengen area without internal border control. The Schengen Protocol sets out that Ireland is not bound by the Schengen acquis, but that it may request to take part in some or all of its provisions. In 2000, Ireland submitted a request to participate in certain non-border related provisions of the Schengen acquis, covering police and judicial cooperation in criminal matters, the fight against irregular migration, drugs, and the law enforcement related part of the Schengen Information System. Ireland did not ask to participate in the parts of the Schengen acquis governing internal and external borders, visa, free movement of third-country nationals and return. Council accepted Ireland's request in 2002 (Council Decision 2002/192/EC), but that decision was only put into effect two decades later (Council Decision (EU) 2020/1745 and Commission Implementing Decision (EU) 2023/201). Schengen acts adopted after 2002 should always contain a recital which either specifies that this new act "constitutes a development of the provisions of the Schengen acquis in which Ireland does not take part, in accordance with Council Decision 2002/192/EC" or which spells out, if Ireland takes part, that "Ireland is taking part, in accordance with Article 5(1) of Protocol No 19 on the Schengen acquis integrated into the framework of the European Union, annexed to the TEU and to the TFEU and Article 6(2) of Council Decision 2002/192/EC". As regards the participation of Ireland in eu-LISA, Council accepted, in 2012 (with Council Decision 2012/764/EU) and subsequently in 2019 (with Council Decision 2019/1749) the request of Ireland to extend its Schengen participation under the Schengen Protocol by taking part in the eu-LISA Regulation (EU) 2018/1726, even though that Agency also deals with parts of the Schengen acquis in which Ireland does not take part (Entry-Exit System, ETIAS, VIS, SIS-border and return).

A (non-authentic) list of the acts that apply to Ireland by virtue of Council Decision 2002/192/EC is maintained by the Irish Department of Justice and can be accessed under the heading "EU Measures that automatically apply to Ireland by virtue of Council Decision 2002/192/EC" at its website: https://www.gov.ie/en/policy-information/105ad-european-affairs/ (accessed in May 2024).

The question whether the Schengen Protocol allowed the UK (which was, before Brexit, in a similar position than Ireland) to selectively participate in certain Schengen acts that were not covered by the partial Schengen participation authorised by the respective Council decision, was subject of three judgements of the European Court of Justice in which the Court highlighted the conception and functioning of the Schengen acquis as coherent ensemble. The refusal of Council to allow the UK to take part in the Frontex Regulation (subject of case C-77/05), in the Regulation on security features for passports and travel documents (subject of case C-137/05) and in the Visa Information System (subject of case C-482/08) was considered by the Court as justified, since these three legal acts were not covered by the areas of the Schengen acquis into which the UK had opted in. The Court made clear that a selective pick-and-choose, going beyond the authorised partial participation

4.2 The Position of Ireland

was not possible, because of the need for maintaining coherence of the relevant Schengen acquis.

Which Protocol defines the relation between Ireland and the Schengen acquis? The Schengen Protocol or the UK/Ireland Protocol?
The participation of Ireland in the Schengen acquis is regulated in the Schengen Protocol. The participation of Ireland in the area of freedom, security, and justice in general, is regulated in the UK/Ireland Protocol. The Schengen Protocol is *lex specialis* and it applies whenever an act is considered Schengen-related, whereas the UK/Ireland Protocol is *lex generalis* and it applies for all non-Schengen related measures adopted in the field of freedom, security, and justice.

Are there two different versions of the Schengen Protocol?
Yes. The 1997 Schengen Protocol was amended and also given a different number in 2009. This may create confusion. Originally the Schengen Protocol was called *Protocol (No 2) integrating the Schengen acquis into the framework of the European Union (1997)* and it consisted of eight Articles. Protocol 1 to the Lisbon Treaty amended the text of the Schengen Protocol and since 1.12.2009 a new version is in force. That new version is called *Protocol (No 19) on the Schengen acquis integrated into the framework of the European Union* and it consists of seven Articles. It is important to always verify, to which version of the Schengen Protocol reference is made, since the numbering of the Articles of the Schengen Protocol and the numbering of paragraphs within the same Articles of the Schengen Protocol was changed.

Are there two different versions of the UK/Ireland Protocol?
Yes. The 1997 UK/Ireland Protocol was amended and also given a different number in 2009. This may create confusion. Originally the UK/Ireland Protocol was called *Protocol (No 4) on the position of the United Kingdom and Ireland (1997)*, and it consisted of eight Articles. Protocol 1 to the Lisbon Treaty amended the text of the UK/Ireland Protocol and since 1.12.2009 a new version is in force. That new version is called *Protocol (No 21) on the position of the United Kingdom and Ireland in respect of the area of freedom, security and justice* and it consists of ten Articles, including a new Article 4a. It is important to always verify, to which version of the UK/Ireland Protocol reference is made, since the numbering of the Articles of the UK/Ireland Protocol and the numbering of paragraphs within the same Articles of the UK/Ireland Protocol was changed.

Do the "Ireland recitals" always contain the latest info on Irish participation?
Not always. The recitals only reflect the situation at the moment of the publication of the legal act. Subsequent developments may affect Irish participation and it is therefore necessary to always cross-check the information contained in the recitals. *Examples*: Recital 53 of the eu-LISA Regulation (EU) 2018/1726 states that Ireland does not participate, but the subsequent Council Decision 2019/1749 authorised Irish participation. Recital 71 of the Eurojust Regulation (EU) 2018/1727 indicates that Ireland does not participate, but Commission Decision (EU) 2019/2006 informs about the participation of Ireland, following receipt of a subsequent notification of Irish intention to participate.

Which types of "Ireland recitals" exist, and what do they imply?
There are several possibilities:

- If the legal act is considered *Schengen-related and if it falls outside the partial Schengen participation* of Ireland, the recital may be formulated like this: *"This Regulation constitutes a development of the provisions of the Schengen acquis in which Ireland does not take part, in accordance with Council Decision 2002/192/EC; Ireland is therefore not taking part in the adoption of this Regulation and is not bound by it or subject to its application."*
- If the legal act is considered *Schengen-related and if it falls within the partial Schengen participation* of Ireland, the recital may be formulated like this: *"Ireland is taking part in this Regulation in accordance with Article 5(1) of Protocol No 19 annexed to the TEU and to the TFEU and Article 6(2) of Council Decision 2002/192/EC."*
- If the legal act is considered *non-Schengen-related* and if it falls *within the scope of Part Three, Title V* of the Treaty (area of freedom, security and justice) the recital may be formulated like this: *"In accordance with Article 3 of the Protocol on the position of the United Kingdom and Ireland, ..., Ireland has given notice by ... of its wish to participate in the adoption and application of this Directive (or: Ireland is not taking part in the adoption of this Directive, and is not bound by or subject to its application."*
- If the legal act is *neither considered Schengen-related nor considered as falling within the scope of Part Three, Title V* of the Treaty (area of freedom, security, and justice) the recitals should contain no specific mentioning of Ireland, and Ireland is bound as a "normal" Member State.

In the (very exceptional) cases of *hybrid legal acts* (see above Sect. 3.2.13) references to both the Schengen Protocol and the UK/Ireland Protocol may be found within the recitals of the same legal act.

4.3 The Position of Denmark

The position of Denmark, in relation to the Schengen acquis, needs to be understood against the historical background of the Danish referendum on the Maastricht Treaty in 1992 that resulted in a strong Danish request not to be bound by supranational EC law in the field of Justice and Home Affairs. At the same time, Denmark wanted to be part of the Schengen area without internal border control. The 1997 Protocol on the position of Denmark reconciled these seemingly incompatible policy aspirations, by using a hitherto unseen legal construction: Denmark was given a broad opt-out in the field of Justice and Home Affairs and it was allowed, at the same time, to implement the Schengen *acquis* in its national law under a sui generis legal construction: Each time, an initiative building upon the Schengen acquis is adopted, Denmark may decide, within 6 months, to implement it, and this measure then creates an obligation under international law between Denmark and the other Member States. If Denmark decides not to do so, "appropriate measures" shall be taken. In practice, Denmark has so far consistently decided to implement in its national law all measures building upon the Schengen acquis (Peers, 2014, p. 34). One consequence of this very unusual legal construction is that the normal EU procedures on enforcement of Union law (infringement procedures and references to the European Court of Justice) cannot be launched vis-à-vis Denmark, if they relate to provisions of the Schengen *acquis*.

The Denmark Protocol has one exception: It does not apply to Schengen measures determining the third countries whose nationals must be in possession of a visa and measures relating to a uniform format for visas. As regards such measures, Denmark is treated and participates like a "normal" Member State (see historical explanations above in Sect. 2.4.3). This exception can be explained by the fact that EC competence to regulate that subject matter had already existed and was exercised before the Amsterdam Treaty (Article 100c EC, which provided for EC competence to determine the third countries whose nationals must be in possession of a visa when crossing the external borders of the Member States and to adopt measures relating to a uniform format for visas, had already been included by the Maastricht Treaty). The Visa List Regulation (EU) 2018/1806 therefore has no specific Denmark recital (*explanation*: This Regulation determines the third countries whose nationals must be in possession of a visa and therefore falls under the exception of Article 6 of the Denmark Protocol. As a consequence, Denmark participates as "normal" Member State), whereas the Visa Code Regulation (EC) No 810/2009 has a Denmark recital, that relates to the Denmark Protocol and Schengen-relatedness (*explanation*: The Visa Code determines procedures for issuing visa, but doesn't determine third countries whose nationals must be in possession of a visa. It therefore doesn't fall under the exception of Article 6 of the Denmark Protocol and Denmark therefore participates only under international law, as foreseen in the Schengen-related provisions of the Denmark Protocol). Likewise, in todays EU visa waiver agreements (containing rules on the third countries whose nationals must be in possession of visas) Denmark participates like a normal Member State, whereas it does not participate in visa facilitation agreements (containing rules on facilitated issuance of visa). However, the latter normally contain a joint declaration, setting out the intention to conclude a parallel bilateral agreement in similar terms with Denmark.

It is important to bear in mind that, as already set out in Sects. 2.6.4 and 2.8, Denmark took part, until 2009, in the adoption of all third pillar JHA instruments covering the policy fields of police and judicial cooperation (such as the European Arrest Warrant Framework Decision 2002/584/JHA, the Prüm II Framework Decision 2008/615/JHA or the Europol Decision 2009/371/JHA) and that Denmark was bound by these instruments like any other Member State, and that the revised Denmark Protocol allowed Denmark to continue applying these instruments also after 2009. Under the terms of the revised Denmark Protocol, Denmark cannot, however, participate in post-Lisbon developments in these fields, unless these constitute a development of the Schengen acquis. As a result, Denmark may gradually become excluded in the future, as these instruments develop further, and may not be covered any more by the "continuation" clause of Article 2 of the Denmark Protocol as amended by the Lisbon Treaty.

This being said, it is important to underline that the abovementioned "exclusion" of Denmark is self-imposed and that Denmark may, at any time, avail itself of the options under either Article 7 or Article 8 of the Denmark Protocol to participate more broadly in the EUs freedom, security and justice acquis.

As explained in more detail below, in Sects. 4.6 (Schengen associated States) and 4.9 (Faroe Islands and Greenland), Denmark always insisted on maintaining its special relationship with other Scandinavian countries and territories bound by the provisions of the Nordic Passport Union and insisted that the functioning of the Nordic Passport Union should not be hampered. A clause (Article 6) was therefore integrated in the Schengen Protocol, providing the basis for the Schengen Association of Norway and Iceland and Article 5(2) of the Danish Schengen Accession Agreement provided for the absence of border checks for persons travelling between the Faroe Islands or Greenland and Schengen States.

Which Protocol defines the relation between Denmark and the Schengen acquis? The Schengen Protocol or the Denmark Protocol?
The pre-Lisbon version of the Schengen Protocol had addressed some aspects of the applicability of the Schengen acquis to Denmark. Since the entry into force of the Lisbon Treaty, the participation of Denmark in the Schengen acquis is entirely regulated in the Denmark Protocol and the Schengen Protocol only contains a cross-reference, in its Article 3, to the Denmark Protocol.

4.3 The Position of Denmark

Are there two different versions of the Denmark Protocol?
Yes. The Denmark Protocol exists in two different versions. This may create confusion. Originally the Denmark Protocol was called *Protocol (No 5) on the position of Denmark (1997)*, and it consisted of seven Articles. Protocol 1 to the Lisbon Treaty amended the text of the Denmark Protocol and since 1.12.2009 a new version is in force. That new version is called *Protocol (No 22) on the position of Denmark*, and it consists of nine Articles (including a new Article 2a) and a new Annex. It is important to always verify to which version of the Denmark Protocol reference is made, since the numbering of the Articles of the Denmark Protocol and the numbering of paragraphs within the same Articles of the Denmark Protocol was changed.

Which types of "Denmark recitals" exist, and what do they imply?
There are several possibilities:

- If the legal act is considered *Schengen-related* and if it falls *within the scope of Part Three, Title V* of the Treaty (area of freedom, security and justice) the recital may be formulated like this: "*In accordance with Articles 1 and 2 of Protocol No 22 on the position of Denmark, annexed to the TEU and to the TFEU, Denmark is not taking part in the adoption of this Regulation and is not bound by it or subject to its application. Given that this Regulation builds upon the Schengen acquis, Denmark shall, in accordance with Article 4 of that Protocol, decide within a period of six months after the Council has decided on this Regulation whether it will implement it in its national law.*"
- If the legal act is considered *Schengen-related*, but if it falls under the exception of Article 6 of the Denmark Protocol (*visa-list and uniform format for visas*): No recital on Denmark since Denmark participates as "normal" Member State.
- If the legal act is considered *non-Schengen-related* and if it falls *within the scope of Part Three, Title V* of the Treaty (area of freedom, security and justice) the recital may be formulated like this: *In accordance with Articles 1 and 2 of Protocol No 22 on the position of Denmark, annexed to the TEU and to the TFEU, Denmark is not taking part in the adoption of this Regulation and is not bound by it or subject to its application.*

4.4 The Position of New Member States

The admission of new Member States to the Schengen area without internal border control requires a high degree of mutual trust. Existing Members need to be reassured that new Members will protect the common external borders and apply the related rules and flanking measures as coherently and diligently as they themselves are required. New Members also need to be given a phasing-in period, during which they can demonstrate to be able to correctly implement these rules and operate the Schengen-related IT systems. For this reason, it became an established practice, formalised in the relevant Acts of Accession, to apply a two-step process leading to the lifting of internal border controls with new Members. The most important feature of this two-step process is the distinction between *"bindingness"* and *"applicability"* of the Schengen acquis. According to the Acts of Accession, new Members are *bound* by the entire Schengen acquis from the date of accession, but not all the Schengen acquis becomes *applicable* from that date. In fact, the Schengen acquis is split into two groups of provisions: Those which are not directly related to the lifting of internal border control—and those which are. The first group of measures becomes *applicable* immediately, while the second one (related to the lifting of internal border control) only becomes applicable once Council has decided unanimously, after verification in accordance with the applicable Schengen evaluation procedures, that the necessary conditions for the application of all parts of the acquis concerned have been met in that State. Pending that decision, the internal borders between old and new Members, where border control has not yet been lifted, remain *de facto* external borders. The first group of measures (binding and applicable immediately) is also referred to, in recitals of relevant legal acts, as *"building upon, or otherwise related to, the Schengen acquis within, respectively, the meaning of Article 3(1) of the 2003 Act of Accession, Article 4(1) of the 2005 Act of Accession and Article 4(1) of the 2011 Act of Accession"*. The second group of measures (binding but not applicable immediately) is also referred to, in recitals of relevant legal acts, as *"building upon, or otherwise related to, the Schengen acquis within, respectively, the meaning of Article 3(2) of the 2003 Act of Accession, Article 4(2) of the 2005 Act of Accession and Article 4(2) of the 2011 Act of Accession"*.

The splitting of the Schengen acquis into two groups of measures, with a temporarily differing scope of territorial application, leads to practical difficulties and opens manifold legal questions, notably in the context of the Schengen large scale IT systems. A telling example of the arising issues was the debate, which emerged, in the negotiations of the Entry-Exit System Regulation, on the applicability of the "90 days in any 180-days period rule" to the territory of both old and new Schengen States (see Council Legal Service Opinion in Council document 13491/16).

The period between accession (to Schengen/EU) and lifting of internal border control varies and has so far lasted between 3 years (for Austria) and more than 9 years (for Croatia). Romania and Bulgaria have been waiting since 2007 until internal border control was (partly) lifted in 2024 and Cyprus is still waiting since 2004. The criterion fixed by the Accession Treaty that *"the necessary conditions for the application of all parts of the acquis concerned shall be met"* reads like a

4.4 The Position of New Member States

technical process, but de facto, thanks also to the unanimity requirement in Council, it is a decision that includes policy assessment. It relates to something which lies at the heart of Schengen, and which escapes a precise legal definition, namely mutual trust.

Is the unanimity requirement for deciding on the full application of the Schengen acquis in a new Member State prescribed by Primary Law?
According to a "Joint Declaration on Article 139", the Convention Implementing the Schengen Agreement shall not be brought into force until the preconditions for its implementation have been fulfilled in the Signatory States and checks at external borders are effective. In Decision SCH/Com-ex(93)10 concerning the declarations by the Ministers and State Secretaries (OJ L 239 of 22.9.2000, pp. 127–128), the Executive Committee confirmed that the "Declaration on Article 139" implies that the bringing into force of the Convention Implementing the Schengen Agreement is subject to an Executive Committee Decision which must be adopted as soon as the preconditions are fulfilled. According to Article 132(2) of the Convention Implementing the Schengen Agreement, the Executive Committee shall take its decisions unanimously. At the occasion of the "Amsterdamisation" of Schengen, a Council statement, attached to Decision 1999/436/EC (OJ L 176, 10.7.1999, p. 30), expressly confirmed that the inclusion of the "Joint Declaration on Article 139" in Decision 1999/436/EC must be *"interpreted as signifying that the decision confirming the capacity of each State acceding to the EU to implement the Schengen acquis, thus permitting the removal of controls at internal frontiers, will be taken unanimously by the Council comprised of the Member States named in Article 1 of the Schengen Protocol."*

All Acts of Accession adopted after the Amsterdamisation of Schengen include a corresponding provision on the two-step approach for joining Schengen, and the requirement for Council to take a unanimous decision on the full application of the Schengen acquis in a new Member State, after consulting the European Parliament. See: Article 3 of the 2003 Act of Accession, Article 4 of the 2005 Act of Accession and Article 4 of the 2011 Act of Accession.

Could future Acts of Accession foresee differing rules for the full application of the Schengen acquis in a new Member State?
Acts of Accession are Primary Law. Nothing prevents Member States and the European Parliament from agreeing differing rules for the full application of the Schengen acquis in a new Member State in future Acts of Accession.

> **How can I find out whether a new Schengen act is applicable (or just binding and not yet applicable) in a Schengen State not yet fully applying the Schengen acquis?**
> Those new Schengen acts which are binding *and applicable* are referred to, in the recitals, as *"building upon, or otherwise related to, the Schengen acquis within, respectively, the meaning of Article 3(1) of the 2003 Act of Accession, Article 4(1) of the 2005 Act of Accession and Article 4(1) of the 2011 Act of Accession"*. The second group of measures (binding but *not applicable* immediately) are referred to, in the recitals, as *"building upon, or otherwise related to, the Schengen acquis within, respectively, the meaning of Article 3(2) of the 2003 Act of Accession, Article 4(2) of the 2005 Act of Accession and Article 4(2) of the 2011 Act of Accession"*.

4.5 The Position of Cyprus

The specific situation of Cyprus is characterised by its division in two parts. The ("Green") line between the areas under the effective control of Cyprus and those areas in which Cyprus does not exercise effective control is subject of a special legal regime, defined by Regulation (EC) No 866/2004 on a regime under Article 2 of Protocol No 10 of the 2003 Act of Accession. The application of this regime poses recurrent legal challenges, when drafting and applying Schengen legal instruments. A recent example are the negotiations of the proposed Screening Regulation, where it had to be clarified, in a recital, whether the external borders related provisions of this instrument apply to the Green Line, even though it does not formally constitute an external border (Recital 51a in Council document 10585/22).

4.6 The Position of Schengen Associated States

4.6.1 Schengen Association Agreements

Norway, Iceland, Switzerland, and Liechtenstein are bound by the Schengen acquis and participate in decision-shaping of new Schengen-related acts through the Mixed Committee, established by their Schengen Association Agreements. It must be underlined that no other Association Agreement has granted similarly far-reaching decision-shaping rights to third States, not even the EEA agreement (Filliez et al., 2008, p. 148).

Norway and Iceland had been, together with Denmark, Finland, and Sweden, already members of the Nordic Passport Union and had abandoned, since 1958, internal passport controls at their internal borders. When Sweden, Finland and

Denmark signed up to Schengen in 1996, their Accession Treaties referred to the need to preserve the Nordic Passport Union. Norway and Iceland were given associate Schengen membership in 1996, and the Schengen Protocol required Council to conclude a Schengen Association Agreement, which was signed in 1999. All five Nordic countries lifted internal border controls with other Schengen States simultaneously and started fully applying the Schengen acquis in March 2001.

The association of Switzerland was part of a political process, linked to the geographical position of the Swiss Confederation and the risk, perceived by Switzerland, of becoming an "island of insecurity" and "country of last asylum" within Schengen (Filliez et al., 2008, p. 155). There was also a strong EU interest in better cooperation with Switzerland in the field of tax evasion. The Swiss Schengen Association Agreement was concluded in 2004, together with an agreement to combat fraud in the area of indirect taxes, as part of the so called "bilateral agreements II" package.

The Schengen accession of Liechtenstein was considered as closely linked to the Swiss Schengen association, due to its geographic position and due to the fact that an open border policy for the movement of persons had existed between Liechtenstein and Switzerland for decades. Article 16 of the Swiss Schengen Association Agreement allowed Liechtenstein to accede to the Swiss Schengen Association agreement. This provision avoided the conclusion of a separate association agreement and thus the creation of a third Mixed Committee (Filliez et al., 2008, p. 169). The Liechtenstein Protocol, concluded in 2008, contains all the essential provisions and has its own termination clauses that are independent from the Swiss agreement. While the Swiss Schengen Association Agreement became fully applicable in 2008, due to the reluctance of some EU Member States in the Council connected to tax cooperation, Liechtenstein was only able to fully join as Schengen member in December 2011.

4.6.2 Operation of the Agreements

The way in which these Schengen Association agreements operate is similar: The already existing Schengen acquis is listed in an annex to the agreement and accepted by the associated States upon signature. The associated States also oblige themselves to accept future measures amending or building upon this acquis. Experts from associated States are allowed to participate in decision-shaping in the same way as Member States expert (presence at Commission expert groups and Council working groups convened in Mixed Committee format), but they cannot take part in the decision itself. Once adopted, Schengen acts are notified and need to be formally accepted by the Associated States. In case of non-acceptance, the Association Agreement shall be considered terminated, unless the Mixed Committee "decides otherwise". Until now this "guillotine clause" was never used. There are also no precedents of the Mixed Committee having "decided otherwise" in such context. The Commission cannot launch infringement procedures against Schengen Associated States. In the case of a dispute about the correct application or interpretation of the Schengen acquis the matter may, however, be added to the agenda of the Mixed Committee. If the dispute cannot be settled by the Mixed Committee, the agreement shall be terminated. Until now, also this "nuclear option" was never used. In practice, it seems, all disputes could already be settled at lower, administrative level. This may be explained by the fact that the adaptational pressure which arises from the potential activation of the termination clause is very strong (Wichmann, 2006, p. 102).

4.6.3 Interlinkage Between Different Schengen Association Agreements

At first glance, the construction of Schengen Association Agreements may seem reasonably simple, but a closer look reveals the high legal complexity and the snowball effect of each further State joining: The smooth operation of the Schengen acquis requires that each Schengen Association Agreements is applied simultaneously with flanking parallel agreements or arrangements binding in those other States which are not directly bound by that Association Agreement. In the case of Switzerland, this implied that a separate agreement between Switzerland and Iceland/Norway as well as between Switzerland and Denmark had to be concluded. Moreover, the relation between Switzerland and UK/Ireland had to be clarified as regards the UK/Irish (limited) scope of participation in the Schengen acquis.

4.6.4 Interlinkage Between Schengen Association Agreements and Dublin/Eurodac Acquis

In addition—and this adds a further layer of technical complication—the Schengen acquis is considered so strongly linked to the Dublin/Eurodac acquis (see above Sect. 3.3.2), that it should only be implemented hand in hand with a series of parallel Dublin/Eurodac Association agreements. This is expressly stated in Article 7 of the Norway/Iceland Schengen Association Agreement and Article 15(4) of the Swiss Schengen Association Agreement.

4.6.5 Interlinkage Between Schengen Association Agreements and Free Movement Acquis

Moreover, as explained above in Sect. 3.3.3, the abolition of internal border control presupposes, as business basis, the existence of harmonised rules on the free movement of persons. Therefore, any third country wishing to be associated to Schengen needed to accept and apply the EU free movement acquis beforehand, as a precondition for being associated to Schengen. The Schengen associated states are bound to apply the relevant EU free movement acquis via the EEA agreement (for Norway, Iceland, and Liechtenstein) and via the 1999 Agreement on the Free Movement of Persons (for Switzerland).

The above mentioned interlinkages imply that any (potential) new Schengen Association Agreement would require the conclusion of more than ten new international agreements: Four agreements on Schengen Association (with EU, with Denmark, with Norway/Iceland, with Switzerland/Liechtenstein), four on Dublin/Eurodac association (with EU, with Denmark, with Norway/Iceland, with Switzerland/Liechtenstein) and a number of further agreements ensuring the application of the EU free movement rules in relations between the new Schengen Associated State and EU States as well as other Schengen Associated States.

4.7 Outermost Regions

4.7.1 *French and Dutch Outermost Regions*

According to its Article 138, the rules of the Schengen Implementing Convention shall only apply to the European territory of France and the Netherlands, thus excluding from the scope of application of Schengen acquis those non-European outermost regions in which, otherwise, Union law is applied in accordance with Article 349 TFEU. Therefore, Schengen rules are not applicable in Martinique, Mayotte, Guadeloupe, French Guiana and Réunion.

4.7.2 *Spanish and Portuguese Outermost Regions*

No comparable exception to the full applicability of Schengen rules is provided for the Spanish and Portuguese outermost regions, and Schengen rules are therefore fully applicable in the Canary Islands, Madeira, and Acores.

4.8 Microstates

4.8.1 *Historically Grown Practices*

The Microstates Andorra, San Marino, Monaco, and Vatican are "islands" within the territory of Schengen States. The way in which the Schengen acquis is applied to these countries is based on established, historically grown practices, predating the Schengen agreements, and in some cases also on bi- and trilateral agreements with neighbouring Schengen States. These established practices survived de facto the advent of the Schengen area, even though the Microstates states were not formally associated and borders with them should in theory have been considered 'external' borders of the EU (Maiani, 2019, p. 87). In addition to enjoying de facto inclusion in the Schengen area, citizens of these Microstates benefit from a series of express unilateral decisions by the EU legislator: They are exempt from the obligation to carry a visa, from the stamping of their passports and from the application of the newly established EU 'entry/exit system', whenever they cross Schengen external borders. A "pragmatic" approach has also been agreed by the Council's Strategic Committee on Immigration, Frontiers and Asylum (SCIFA) in 2004 which provides that citizens of Andorra and San Marino may use EU lanes at Schengen external border crossing points (Council document 13020/04). These practices, which may be partly considered *praeter legem* or even *contra legem*, pose legal challenges which are likely to become more visible when future IT systems (Entry-Exit System, ETIAS and new VIS) will become operational.

What are SCIFA documents?
The Strategic Committee on Immigration, Frontiers and Asylum (SCIFA) is a Council group, set up by Coreper, to prepare the Council's discussions with regard to immigration, frontiers and asylum. The tasks of SCIFA, consisting of senior officials, is to issue strategic guidelines in matters relating to immigration, frontiers and asylum and to give substantive input to Coreper's discussions. Details on the nature of SCIFA are set out in Council document 17476/10.

Are SCIFA documents legally binding?
No. Due to their nature (non-legislative Council documents) SCIFA conclusions and recommendations cannot be legally binding. SCIFA documents may, however, reflect a joint understanding of Member States on the interpretation and implementation of Union law and can therefore be qualified as "soft law".

4.8.2 *Monaco*

There are currently (in 2024) no border checks between France and Monaco. Both French and Monegasque authorities oversee joint border checks at Monegasque external border crossing points (port and heliport). Building on a bilateral agreement (Convention de voisinage du 18 mai 1963), adapted in 1997 and 2002, the third-country holders of residence permits issued by Monaco can travel freely in the Schengen area for up to 90 days in any 180-day period. To that effect, Monaco can only issue a residence permit following a binding opinion delivered by the French authorities. France produces residence permits for Monaco, in the uniform format (i.e., with security features), and following a binding opinion of France, Monaco authorities issue them. Based on a decision of the Executive Committee of 23 June 1998 (SCH/Com-ex (98) 19), Monegasque residence permits are notified by France in accordance with the Schengen Borders Code (Article 39) and they are listed among residence permits issued by Member States in Annex 22 of the Practical Handbook for Border Guards.

4.8.3 Andorra

While there is some border infrastructure in place, there are currently (in 2024) no systematic border controls between France/Andorra and between Spain/Andorra. Entry/exit stamps are therefore not systematically affixed on passports of third-country nationals. According to a tripartite convention (Convention entre la République française, le Royaume d'Espagne et la Principauté d'Andorre du 4 décembre 2000 relative à l'entrée, à la circulation, au séjour et à l'établissement de leurs ressortissants), Andorra can only issue residence permits to third-country nationals following an opinion by either France or Spain or following a previous legal residence of at least 1 year in France or Spain. In application of this Convention, the residence permits issued by Andorra are valid for the territories of Andorra, Spain, and France only. In these two Member States, the entry and stay regime of third-country nationals holding a residence permit issued by Andorra is identical to the one of third-country nationals holding a residence permit from France or Spain. Consequently, in application of this Convention, nationals of countries normally requiring a Schengen visa but holding a residence permit issued by Andorra are in practice not subjected to the visa obligation for entry through and stays in France and Spain. However, such persons require a Schengen visa to travel to or through other Member States.

The Association Agreement between the EU and Andorra and San Marino, agreed in 2023, provides for the participation of Andorra and San Marino in the EU's internal market, comparable to that enjoyed by Norway, Iceland and Liechtenstein in application of the Agreement on the European Economic Area. That agreement does not contain border or migration related provisions. In March 2024, the Commission recommended the opening of negotiations on an agreement between the EU and Andorra on several aspects in the field of border management (COM(2024)108). The objective of the envisaged agreement is to provide an appropriate legal basis for the 'de facto' absence of border checks and, as a compensatory measure, to include rules on residence permits and adjustments with regard to the upcoming entry into operation of the Entry/Exit System and the European Travel Information and Authorization System.

4.8.4 San Marino

There are currently (in 2024) no border checks between Italy and San Marino. This can be explained by the close relationship with Italy, predating the establishment of the Schengen area, confirmed by the 1939 Convenzione di Amicizia e Buon Vicinato tra l'Italia e San Marino. The Association Agreement between the EU and Andorra and San Marino, agreed in 2023, provides for the participation of Andorra and San Marino in the EU's internal market, comparable to that enjoyed by Norway, Iceland and Liechtenstein in application of the Agreement on the European Economic Area. That agreement does not contain border or migration related provisions. In March 2024, the Commission recommended the opening of negotiations on an agreement between the EU and San Marino on several aspects in the field of border management (COM(2024)109). The objective of the envisaged agreement is to provide an appropriate legal basis for the 'de facto' absence of border checks and, as a compensatory measure, to include rules on residence permits and adjustments, especially with regard to the upcoming entry into operation of the Entry/Exit System and the European Travel Information and Authorization System.

4.8.5 Vatican/Holy See

There is currently (in 2024) no agreement between the Vatican/Holy See and Italy regarding the residence permits issued by the former and there is no border control between these two States. Third-country nationals residing in the Vatican normally hold either Vatican City State citizenship (thus a passport issued by the Vatican City State) or a diplomatic/service passport of the Holy See. They are therefore exempted from the obligation to hold a visa.

4.9 Faroe Islands and Greenland

Article 5 of the Danish Schengen Accession Agreement stipulates two seemingly contradictory rules: According to Article 5(1) of the Danish Schengen Accession Agreement, the Schengen Implementing Convention does not apply to the Faroe Islands and Greenland. Article 5(2) of the Danish Schengen Accession Agreement prescribes, however, the absence of border checks for persons travelling between the Faroe Islands or Greenland and Schengen States. This provision had been inserted because Greenland and the Faroe Islands are not members of the European Union but covered by the framework of the Nordic Passport Union. A joint declaration attached to the Danish Schengen Accession Agreement specifies that the Accession Agreement shall be brought into force "*once the Executive Committee has established that the rules which it deems necessary for the implementation of effective control and surveillance measures at the external borders of the Faroe Islands and Greenland and the necessary compensatory measures, including the implementation of the Schengen Information System (SIS), have been applied and are effective*". This declaration was substantiated by two Danish memoranda (Council documents 11487/99 and 11488/99), which presented in detail the necessary measures for implementing Article 5(2). The measures listed in these memoranda provide that border checks and border surveillance at the outer borders of the Faroe Islands and Greenland are carried out by the Danish police, on behalf of the Danish authorities, in accordance with the Schengen rules. Danish border guards have access to the SIS and the VIS and can refuse entry to the Faroe Islands and Greenland, based on a SIS alert. A list of those parts of the Schengen acquis which is relevant for that purpose is annexed to the memoranda. This legal construction and notably the fact that Faroes and Greenland are not applying the Schengen visa rules, raises several legal and practical questions. Third-country nationals who travel to Faroes or Greenland may need two types of visas: A Schengen visa for passing Schengen external border control and a separate visa granting a right to stay in Faroes or Greenland. Some of these practical questions are answered in the *Danish government Guidelines No. 9565 of 28 June 2021 on the Processing of Applications for Visas for Denmark* (Visa Guidelines) (pages 89–90). The fact that Denmark is policing Greenland's borders has the effect that the Schengen area now even has a *de facto* external land border with Canada: Following the settlement, in 2022, of a long-standing territorial dispute between Canada and Denmark, Hans Island/Tartupaluk, situated between Greenland and Canada, was split into two parts, with a land border line separating Canadian and Greenland territory of the island.

A still open political debate relates to the question whether local home-rule administration in Greenland and Faroe Islands may take over some or all Schengen border control related tasks from Danish authorities.

4.10 Foreign Military Bases

Schengen law does not know any general fiction of extraterritoriality, applicable to third-country military bases situated on Schengen territory. International arrivals and departures at these bases should therefore, as a rule, be subject to border checks in accordance with the Schengen Borders Code. These border checks may, however, be subject to facilitations set out in the NATO Troup Statute of 1951 (pre-existing international law, applicable before Schengen Borders Code entered into force), including standardised "NATO travel/mission orders" and holiday certificates ("authority for leave"), covering weekend trips outside the military base and allowing for derogations from stamping. There are also templates for special IDs. Moreover, the facilitation provided in annex VII.4 of the Schengen Borders Code for third-country holders of official or service passports may be applicable, entailing priority treatment and an exemption from the requirement to prove means of subsistence/establish the purpose of travel.

4.11 UK Sovereign Base Areas of Akrotiri and Dhekelia

The situation is entirely different for the UK Sovereign Base Areas (SBAs) of Akrotiri and Dhekelia, situated in Cyprus. These SBAs are overseas territory of the UK and the border line between Cyprus and the SBAs is therefore an external border within the meaning of the Schengen Borders Code. However, according to EU law (Article 5 of Protocol No 3 Annexed to Cyprus' Act of Accession and Article 7(5) of the Protocol relating to the Sovereign Base Areas of the UK in Cyprus, annexed to the 2019 Withdrawal Agreement), there shall be no checks on persons at land and sea boundaries between SBAs and Cyprus. This provision builds upon historically grown arrangements which had been in place since 1960 with the aim of avoiding any kind of frontier post between Cyprus and the SBAs so that the civilian population can move freely between the two (Adams, 2021, pp. 501–502). To compensate for the absence of controls between the SBAs and Cyprus, Article 7(2) of the Protocol relating to the Sovereign Base Areas of the UK in Cyprus requires the SBA authorities to exercise controls at designated external border crossing points so that only persons entitled to be admitted to Cyprus in accordance with the SBA Protocol may cross the external frontier of the SBAs. In practice, the only external border crossing points within the SBAs are the military airport in the Akrotiri SBA, SBA seaports and the two crossing points Strovilia and Pergamos on the green line between the Dhekelia SBA and Northern Cyprus, as specified in Article 7(6) of the Protocol relating to the Sovereign Base Areas of the UK in Cyprus. The entry requirements to be checked by SBA authorities are listed in Article 7(3) of the Protocol relating to the Sovereign Base Areas of the UK in Cyprus, and are partly (but not entirely) identical with the entry requirements under the Schengen Borders Code. This legal construction is unique in the Schengen area, insofar as it delegates the conduct of border checks and the resulting authorisation to enter the territory of a Schengen State (given that there are no further checks on persons moving between Cyprus and the SBAs) to third-country (UK-SBA) authorities. The (potential) migratory and security risk for other Schengen States emanating from this legal construction is, however, for the moment limited, since Cyprus is not yet member of the area without internal border control.

4.12 Ceuta and Melilla

As regards the cities of Ceuta and Melilla (Spanish exclaves situated in northern Africa and surrounded by Moroccan territory), Schengen rules are applicable, but several specific rules apply which are defined in a Declaration on the towns of Ceuta and Melilla attached to the 1991 Spanish Schengen Accession Agreement. This declaration provides for continued entry checks on persons arriving from Ceuta/Melilla to Schengen States, continued exit checks for passengers departing from Ceuta/Melilla to Schengen States, continued application of pre-existing local border traffic arrangements between Ceuta/Melilla and neighbouring Moroccan provinces and a continued possibility to issue visa limited to Ceuta/Melilla territory to Moroccan nationals.

4.13 Kaliningrad

With the 2004 enlargement of the EU, Kaliningrad became an enclave between Schengen States. In preparation of the 2004 enlargement, the topic of transit was high on the political agenda and its resolution an important political parameter for Lithuania's accession to the EU. At the 11 November 2002 EU Russia summit, both sides agreed on a "Joint EU-Russia Statement on Transit between Kaliningrad and the rest of the Russian Federation", which fixed the frame for a special transit scheme which was subsequently cast into EU law by means of two Council Regulations adopted in April 2003. Regulations (EC) No 693/2003 (transit scheme) and 694/2003 (specimen of transit documents) created a facilitated Schengen transit scheme for travel of "third-country nationals who must necessarily cross the territory of one or several Member States in order to travel between two parts of their own country which are not geographically contiguous" (i.e. Russians travelling to and from the Kaliningrad Area of the Russian Federation), and special documents were introduced (notably the Facilitated Transit Document and the Facilitated Rail Transit Document) from 1 July 2003. Holders of these transit documents are checked at the borders when transiting Schengen States, but they need not hold visa. According to Protocol No 5 on the transit of persons by land between the region of Kaliningrad and other parts of the Russian Federation annexed to the 2003 Accession Treaty, the Lithuanian costs for the operation of the Kaliningrad Transit Scheme, are borne by the EU budget. Moreover, in 2011, the Schengen rules on local border traffic were amended in view of the exceptional geographic situation of Kaliningrad: With Regulation (EU) No 1342/2011 amending Regulation (EC) No 1931/2006, the entire Kaliningrad oblast and certain Polish administrative districts were included in the border areas eligible for facilitated local border traffic.

4.14 Mount Athos

As part of Greece, the self governed Aghion Oros (Mount Athos) is part of the Schengen Area. A Joint Declaration concerning Mount Athos, attached to the 1992 Agreement on the Accession of the Hellenic Republic to the Convention Implementing the Schengen Agreement, states that the special status granted to Mount Athos, as guaranteed by Article 105 of the Hellenic Constitution and the Charter of Mount Athos, will be taken into account in the application and subsequent preparation of new provisions of Schengen rules. This declaration, which mirrors a similar joint declaration annexed to the 1979 Greek EC Accession Treaty, was aimed at reassuring those who were worried that the centuries-old prohibition on the admittance of women as well as the traditional right to offer sanctuary to people from orthodox countries would be at risk because of joining Schengen. This declaration is of political nature and does not provide for concrete derogations from Schengen rules.

4.15 Åland Islands

According to Article 355(4) TFEU the provisions of the Treaties shall apply to the Åland Islands in accordance with the provisions set out in Protocol 2 to the 1994 Act of Accession of Finland, Sweden, and Austria to the EU. Protocol 2 provides for some derogations on acquisition of real property and excise duties, but no derogation relating to the applicability of the Schengen acquis. In a declaration made by Finland in the context of its 1996 Schengen Accession Treaty, Finland nevertheless stated that obligations resulting from Protocol 2 shall be complied with, when implementing the 1990 Schengen Implementing Convention.

4.16 Svalbard (Spitzbergen)

Article 14 of the Norwegian Schengen Association Agreement states clearly that it does not apply to Svalbard (Spitzbergen). For this reason, flights from a Schengen State to Svalbard are not considered Schengen internal flights, and border checks need to be carried out at Schengen airports upon arrival from (or departure to) Svalbard.

4.17 Gibraltar

Due to the UKs non-participation in Schengen, the border between Spain and Gibraltar (an overseas territory of the UK) had always been an external border of the Schengen area, and movements of persons between Spain and Gibraltar had been subject to external border control even before the withdrawal of the UK from the EU.

The exact physical location of the external border between Spain and Gibraltar has been subject of centuries of legal and political debate. Annex 4 to the Practical Handbook for Border Guards lists "La Línea de la Concepción" as an external land border crossing point between Gibraltar and Spain, with the remark: *"The customs post and police checkpoint at "La Línea de la Concepción" does not correspond to the outline of the border as recognised by Spain in the (1713) Treaty of Utrecht."* Due to the controversy on the demarcation of the borders of Gibraltar a special derogation was included in Article 70(8) of the Frontex Regulation (EU) 2019/1896, suspending its application to the borders of Gibraltar *"until the date on which an agreement is reached on the scope of the measures concerning the crossing by persons of the external borders."* This derogation in the Frontex Regulation relates to Frontex measures only. All other external border instruments of the Schengen acquis are applicable at the Spanish-Gibraltar land border.

Brexit had an impact on the situation at the Spanish/Gibraltar border crossing point, in so far as UK nationals are not considered EU citizens anymore and need to undergo Schengen entry and exit checks applicable to third-country nationals, including, once it will be operational, registration in the Entry and Exit System. Due to Gibraltar's geographical proximity and economic interdependence with the Union, there are high numbers of daily border crossings which pose administrative challenges. In view of this challenge, the Commission recommended to Council in July 2021 (COM(2021)411), to authorise the opening of negotiations for an agreement between EU and the UK, in respect of Gibraltar.

The aim of the envisaged agreement is to remove the current physical border structures while nevertheless maintaining that Gibraltar would not become part of the Schengen area without control at internal borders nor of the Customs Union. To ensure a full protection of the Schengen area, external border control and surveillance would take place at Gibraltar port, airport and waters, carried out by Spain, applying the relevant EU rules. The Border Crossing points to be established at port and airport would allow the application of the relevant EU legislation including the implementation and use of databases necessary for border checks.

The question if, and to what extent, non-Schengen administrations may take over certain (ancillary) Schengen border control tasks (already mentioned above in the context of Greenland/Faroes (Sect. 4.9) and Sovereign Base Areas (Sect. 4.11) is likely to be also a point of discussion in these negotiations).

References

Adams, C. (2021). The withdrawal agreement, protocol relating to the Sovereign base areas of the United Kingdom of Great Britain and Northern Ireland in Cyprus. In T. Liefländer, M. Kellerbauer, & E. Dumitriu-Segnana (Eds.), *The UK–EU withdrawal agreement*. Oxford University Press.

Filliez, F., Martenczuk, B., & Van Thiel, S. (2008). Schengen/Dublin: The association agreements with Iceland, Norway, and Switzerland. In *Justice, liberty, security: New challenges for EU external relations* (pp. 145–183).

Maiani, F. (2019). Unique, yet archetypal: Relations between the European Union and Andorra, Monaco and San Marino. In *The proliferation of privileged partnerships between the European Union and its neighbours* (pp. 84–101). Routledge.

Peers, S. (2014). Denmark and EU justice and home affairs law: Really opting back in? *EU Law Analysis, 8*.

Wichmann, N. (2006). The participation of the Schengen associates: Inside or outside? *European Foreign Affairs Review, 11*(1), 87.

Chapter 5
Outcome of Research Interviews with "Schengen Veterans"

This chapter complements the factual description given in the above chapters. It summarizes the outcome of research interviews conducted in 2022 and 2023 with "Schengen veterans", i.e., officials and practitioners who had (or have) worked for a long time with Schengen issues in European and national administrations, some of them even in the early 1980s and 1990s. The research questions posed to these veterans in semi-structured interviews focused on topics on which few or no replies can be found in official documents or academic literature and included the question "Why were certain subject matters considered as Schengen-related and others not, and why has this distinction changed in the course of years?"

In total, 25 persons with long-standing experience in the field of Schengen were interviewed. Most of these "Schengen veterans" had acquired their experience in periods between 1980 and 2020 within European institutions. A majority had worked at the European Commission and the Council Secretariat, some also at the previous Schengen Secretariat and at the Benelux Secretariat. Some interview partners had followed the development of Schengen from within national administrations. The interviewed persons included four (former) Director Generals, six (former) Directors and five (former) Heads of Unit.

The result of these key informant interviews facilitate understanding of the context of certain legal questions discussed in this book. The replies reflect the consolidated institutional memory of relevant individual actors in the field of Schengen, and they also include recommendations on the way forward for reducing legal complexity.

Why was an intergovernmental approach chosen in the 1980s to realise the abolishment of internal border control?
This question was asked to those interview partners who had already been involved on Schengen matters at an early stage in the 1980s. Most of the replies drew a convergent picture on why an intergovernmental approach (as opposed to a Community approach) was chosen for realising the abolishment of internal border control and

explained that this choice was caused by several interdependent reasons: The (perceived) absence of EC competence for addressing that issue; the position of the UK which blocked any attempts for a harmonised lifting of internal borders at EC level and the absence of a possibility for closer cooperation (under an EC umbrella) for a smaller group of "willing" Member States:

> At that time (1985–1990), the only way for realising abolishment of internal border controls was via an intergovernmental approach, since UK blocked the otherwise necessary unanimity for an EC approach and an option of closer cooperation did not exist yet.

> Schengen can only be explained by a combination of different factors. One primary reason was the absence of EC competencies in that field. Moreover, only few Member States wanted—initially—to be on board and to give up competencies on border related issue (this only changed step-by-step some years after). The UK position and the absence of a possibility for enhanced cooperation were only further reasons, but not the main ones.

Some also pointed to a general feeling of distrust towards Brussels which had been prevailing amongst Member States at that time and a perceived fear at national level of encroaching EC competencies:

> The main explanation was fatigue and frustration of Member States about Brussels. Delors arrived only in 1985, but the Saarbrücken agreement was already concluded in 1984. In that period Member States didn't trust that EC would find appropriate solutions.

> There is a mixed explanation: Distrust vis-a-vis Brussels and fear of encroaching EC competencies.

However, none of the replies indicated that there would have been an express intention of Member States to evade transparency and control by EC institutions. According to the replies, intergovernmentalism was perceived as a correct and right way forward to achieve progress on the matter, within in a smaller group:

> The argument sometimes used that Member States constructed the intergovernmental approach to escape transparency and control by EC institutions was not predominant.

> In that period, the prevailing feeling between Member States was that borders and the substance of Schengen had nothing to do with EC law at all. Thus intergovernmentalism was perceived as correct approach.

Asked, whether it would have been necessary to have recourse to the intergovernmental method for abolishing internal border control in the absence of the UK, replies differed. Some stated that—in the absence of the UK—the other Member States would have probably been able to find the necessary unanimity to abolish internal border control under EC law, others questioned that conclusion and pointed at the prevailing unwillingness by Member States, in that period, to recognise EC competence in this field:

> The UK had been blocking the extension of Article 100a (qualified majority voting) to border/free movement issues in Single European Act and there was no option of enhanced cooperation existing at that time, thus Member States had to use the detour of an intergovernmental approach.

> The choice of the intergovernmental approach was not really the fault of the UK but rather due to the unwillingness by Member States to recognise EC competence in this field.

Why did the Schengen Agreements include certain subject matters and others not?

This question was asked to those interview partners who had been involved on Schengen matters in the 1980s, including those involved in the negotiations of the 1990 Schengen Implementing Convention. Several replies point to the important influence which Benelux rules had on the text of the Schengen Implementing Convention, including striking similarities between Title II of the Convention Implementing the Schengen Agreement and the Benelux rules (applicable in the late 1980s) in relation to the lifting of internal border control, free movement of third-country nationals, external borders, visa etc. This Benelux influence may have been reinforced by the fact that the Benelux secretariat in Brussels, offered secretarial assistance, translation facilities and offices for the evolving Schengen Secretariat and those involved in negotiating and drafting the Schengen Implementing Convention:

> The main substantive input came from the 1960 Benelux Convention and Benelux rules.

> Contrary to academic writing which sometimes states that the main substantive input came from Germany, the reality was that the main input on many key provisions was directly taken from the 1960 Benelux Convention and implementing Benelux rules.

> The Benelux memorandum of 12.12.1984 demonstrates well the Benelux influence on embryonic Schengen. Benelux was one of the main sources of inspiration for the rules set out in the Schengen Implementing Convention. In mainstream public perception, this influence may, however, still be underrated.

Many replies also underline that the text of the Convention Implementing the Schengen Agreement must be understood as the result of intergovernmental negotiations, during which each of the five signing States tried to accommodate its national interests. This relates in particular to the choice of the flanking topics which were included as Schengen-related as well as those that were not:

> It was a deal between the five original signatories, possibly also influenced by topics mentioned in the 1985 Commission White Paper on completing the internal Market (COM(85)310).

> Driven by policy interests of five original Member States. This was sometimes criticised as monopoly and undemocratic approach by the Commission, but it was the historical reality.

As regards the inclusion of the specific subject matters of firearms, drugs, mutual legal assistance, extradition and *ne bis in idem*, one interview partner had precise memories:

> It was a package deal amongst the five original signatories: The five chief negotiators decided as follows on the limitation of subjects to be regulated in the framework of the Schengen Convention: Netherlands, Germany and Luxemburg wanted that Belgium and France changed their laws on the purchase and registration of firearms (it was very easy at that time for criminals to obtain guns in Belgium or rifles in France). Germany, France, Belgium, and Luxemburg wanted the Netherlands to change its policies and practices on narcotic drugs, in particular in relation to cannabis (which could easily be obtained in "coffee shops" in the border regions with Belgium and Germany). Netherlands, Germany, and France wanted Luxemburg to change its laws on the bank secrecy and the fiscal offenses, in

particular to put an end to the Luxemburg practice to refuse systematically all requests for mutual legal assistance and extradition for fiscal offenses, both in matters of direct taxes and of indirect taxes (Luxemburg law distinguished between tax fraud and tax evasion, the latter not being considered unlawful). And Netherlands, supported by France, wanted Germany to change its laws so as to give ne bis in ídem effect to judicial decisions taken in the other partner States (in fact Germany had convicted Dutch nationals for drugs offenses for which they had already been convicted in the Netherlands, which did not please the Dutch).

The subject matter of asylum and legal migration was, in general, considered as too complicated and heavy for including it in the Convention Implementing the Schengen Agreement and therefore it was left to national law. There was, however, one noteworthy exception, namely the determination of responsibility rules for processing asylum applications. These responsibility rules (Articles 28–38 of the Convention Implementing the Schengen Agreement) were designed in view of the single market logic of determining responsible Member States and not in view of harmonising substantive asylum law:

> The Convention Implementing the Schengen Agreement focused on essential elements, it would have made the exercise too complicated to add harmonised rules on asylum or legal migration issues

> The original five Schengen States had no significant external borders. The Convention Implementing the Schengen Agreement was negotiated still in times of cold war and iron curtain. The responsibility rules on asylum seekers (chapter 7) were therefore considered as 'fair'. Only became an issue when Greece joined…

What happened to the first generation (1990–1999) of "lost children of Schengen"?

The replies provided only limited insight. This may be explained by the fact that the question of "Schengen relatedness" had limited practical relevance until 1999, since until that moment all Schengen States were also bound by the relevant developments of EC law and at that time, the prevailing idea was that Schengen was a laboratory and that its rules should—in the long term—gradually be accepted by all Member States in the form of EC/EU law. Nevertheless, some experts commented:

> This is a tricky issue. Dublin, firearms, visa list etc remain part of a "broader political Schengen acquis" but they are now to be applied by all Member States and don't necessarily constitute Schengen acquis within the technical meaning of the Schengen Protocol.

The relationship between the firearms Directive and Schengen acquis was described as an unclear and confusing story, hanging between Schengen-relatedness and non-relatedness:

> There was a not so clear link with Schengen evaluation. Initially, the firearms Directive and its amendment in 2008 were not considered Schengen relevant. Then, after the 2008 amendment, Switzerland was informed by a note of the Council Secretariat that they had to adapt their legislation to bring it in line with the Schengen acquis. The agreements with Liechtenstein and Switzerland mention firearms though it was not mentioned as part of the Schengen acquis. As a result of the note, Switzerland changed its national legislation, mentioning the Schengen acquis. Today everyone seems of the view that it is part of the Schengen acquis, hopefully putting an end to the confusion.

As regards the provisions on responsibility for asylum seekers, the replies highlight two facts, both of which are related to the UK. On the one hand, there was apparently a strong UK interest in being part of the mechanism, which explains why the Dublin Convention was negotiated and agreed upon nearly in parallel to the very similar rules of Articles 28–38 of the Convention Implementing the Schengen Agreement. On the other hand, UK also seemed to have exercised its influence to make sure that Dublin was not considered as Schengen-related in the 1999 definition of the Schengen acquis:

> The fact that Dublin was negotiated in parallel with the Convention Implementing the Schengen Agreement can be explained by strong UK interest to participate in that mechanism

> I had the impression that the position of the UK was part of the reason why Dublin was taken out of the Schengen acquis.

The question of what had happened to the transport chapter of the Convention Implementing the Schengen Agreement (Articles 120–125) could only be answered by one expert:

> I cannot give you an exact reason. I asked myself the same question. When I worked on Schengen cooperation, I have a few times tried to find out for what reasons certain aspects were not considered Schengen relevant. Even people that were actively involved in the discussions did not have clear answers and I was unable to locate any documents that could shed light on it. My best guess in this case is recital 4(d) of Council Decision 1999/435/EC: The subject matter of the provision is covered by and therefore superseded by existing European Community or Union legislation or by a legal act adopted by all Member States.

Why did Member States accept unanimously, in 1999, that Schengen would be integrated into EU?
The replies provided differing explanations, ranging from a perceived fear of legal action, financial considerations, pressure from the European Parliament and Commission as well as the strong policy steer provided by the Netherlands on that issue. The proposed explanations don't exclude each other and may all contain valid points:

> Main reason for integrating Schengen into EU was that Member States feared that Commission would launch legal proceedings following the incorporation of subject matters covered by Schengen in the third pillar by the Maastricht Treaty.

> The main push for the maximalist approach of immediate full integration of the Schengen acquis into EU law came from the Netherlands. Another main driver for the Schengen Protocol were financial considerations (administrative costs for Schengen meetings and interpretation became difficult to finance).

> Push came from the Netherlands, since the Dutch Parliament criticised Schengen for lack of transparency, lack of parliamentary control and lack of judicial oversight.

> One component which facilitated the integration of Schengen into EU was the fact that in the third-pillar, the unanimity requirement continued to be applicable.

What were the reasons for the rather restrictive line in labelling of Schengen-relatedness of legal acts from 1999 onwards?

The replies to this question show a surprising variety. They are convergent in so far as they consider that the developments were rather based on political considerations than on legal considerations. However, not less than five differing political reasons which may have triggered Council to adopt a restrictive approach in the labelling of new legal acts as "Schengen-related" were mentioned:

1. Allowing the UK to participate.

   More interest to have London aboard than Reykjavik.

   The Council approach can be explained by the legitimate concern to have UK aboard in important new JHA instruments.

2. Preventing non-Member States from joining the whole JHA field.

   Reason was that Norway/Iceland and later Switzerland/Liechtenstein should not be allowed to join the whole/broader field of JHA policies without becoming Member States. This was clearly a political choice which was followed from the adoption of Council Decision 99/437 onwards.

   Keeping third countries out was an important consideration. They should become Member States if they wanted to benefit from the developing acquis. Normal EU law, binding on all Member States (as opposed to Schengen law,) should prevail to the extent possible.

3. Accelerate decision-making.

   Avoid time-consuming consultation of Mixed Committee.

   One component which explains the decision to declare the European Arrest Warrant as not Schengen relevant was the urgency under which Member States wanted to adopt that act (referral to the Mixed Committee would have taken too much time).

4. Limit mutual recognition to Member States only

   For the European Arrest Warrant and other mutual recognition instruments, the background was that the UK had pushed strongly (in 1998 Cardiff conclusion and 1999 Tampere conclusions) that the approach of mutual recognition and not of approximation should be followed. When the first mutual recognition instruments were then decided upon, Member States insisted that the UK should also participate (and be given no escape route) (NB: At that time, the Protocols would have allowed UK not to participate if it is Schengen-related, but the Protocols did not give an opt-out option for adopted non-Schengen-related third pillar instruments.) Next to this, France made it clear that it could accept the principle of mutual recognition only insofar as decisions by other Member States (and not third countries) were affected.

5. Limit the number of legal acts which might be applied on instalments (under the two-step approach applicable to Schengen acquis for new Member States).

   Moreover, in view of a large number of new Member States joining soon, Council wanted to avoid increasing the number of legal acts which might possibly only applied on instalments (two step approach applicable to Schengen acquis for new Member States).

As regards the role played by the Council and the Commission in deciding on the Schengen-relatedness of new legal acts, all replies agree that the Council (its Legal

Service) played an important role and that the Commission's attention was rather focused on achieving substantive progress than to fight for maintaining the Schengen-relatedness of its proposals:

> The driving force was indeed the Council Legal Service. The Commission (and its Legal Service) paid only limited attention to the Schengen labelling, since all Commission attention was focused on substantive progress in the newly acquired fields of EU/EC competency.
>
> In the very early days, we had difficulty enough as Commission in making the Member States realise that Schengen was no longer intergovernmental and that it was now bound by Community/Union law and principles.
>
> Commission was not really an active player on the issue of Schengen-relatedness..

Some replies also reflected on the reasons why there was hardly any protest against the restrictive approach on labelling new acts as Schengen-related. It appears that the Schengen Associated States (which were most affected by that approach) flagged some political protest in the beginning, but that they soon accepted the new reality:

> The voice of Norway/Iceland was weak and for Denmark the non labelling as Schengen-related in the field of police cooperation did not pose a problem for as long as third pillar existed.
>
> Switzerland protested, but only at political and not at legal level. There was no possibility to turn to the European Court of Justice and discussion at Mixed Committee level was last resort.
>
> The only ones who were affected were Norway/Iceland and later Switzerland. Switzerland was (later) not so keen on reinforced police and judicial cooperation because of its bank secret (link to its declaration on Art 50 of the Convention Implementing the Schengen Agreement).

What can be done to reduce the legal complexity?

Some interview partner suggested to simply accept the historically grown situation, as it stands today, and questioned both the need and the feasibility to reduce legal complexity:

> Maybe we simply have to live with this historically grown legal complexity?
>
> Difficult to answer. Broadening Schengen relevance may help (from a legal/theoretical point of view), but should this be really done?
>
> There is no one-size-fits-all solution.

Others indicated that a broadening of the concept of Schengen-relatedness which re-oriented itself on the scope of the Schengen Implementing Convention might simplify issues, notably in a post-Brexit political landscape. But some also warned that this would be a free gift for third countries.

> Brexit marks a new era indeed. Added value of labelling more acts as Schengen-related may be existent for Denmark, Switzerland, and Norway.
>
> Added value of labelling more acts as Schengen-related is existent. Practical importance should not be overrated, however, since currently this States are bound in through well working bilaterals, and current practice works smoothly.

Main counterargument against extending concept of Schengen-relatedness is that this would be a free gift for the four Schengen Associated States.

In other replies, a contrary proposal was made, namely, to completely abandon the concept of Schengen acquis, and to treat it just like normal Union law:

> Alternatively, one may think about doing away with special labelling of Schengen acquis and treat it just like normal Union law (with special derogation for Ireland to maintain the Common Travel Area; and involving Schengen Associated States via an extended EEA). The latter would, however, require a change in Primary law.

> I have clear preference for fully assimilating Schengen law to normal Union law. This is the most sustainable approach. Associate States may participate via an EEA like mechanism. Schengen Evaluation could be replaced by a broader "JHA evaluation" under Article 70 TFEU.

Some interview partners presented concrete ideas for reconsidering horizontally and at political level the concept of Schengen-relatedness, with close involvement of the most affected States. Some also suggested that the results of this political process should be subsequently pinned down in horizontal Guidelines or Decisions, tackling the issue in a transparent and binding way for the years to come:

> The "restrictive line" on the scope of the Schengen acquis as expressed in Decision 99/437 has now been applied for 24 years and became part of reality. A change to it would have to be considered jointly by Council, Commission, Denmark, Ireland, and Schengen Associated States (possibly in a friends of Presidency Group) and might be endorsed in the form of a protocol to the Association Agreements containing agreed Guidelines on Schengen-relatedness, endorsed also by Denmark and Ireland for the purposes of their protocols. Such changed approach could arguably take a broader view on the scope of Schengen-relatedness, both for political reasons (argument: it is positive for security if a large group of States apply the same acquis) and for legal reasons (argument: such approach simplifies legal issues and avoids multiplication of flanking bilaterals).

> Council Decision 1999/437/EC is not carved in stone, and it may be changed. It might be useful to now have a fresh look at the subject matters to be considered as Schengen-related in view of reducing legal complexities. This horizontal assessment should take place at a broader/horizontal level, thus avoiding the current piecemeal case-by-case approach. It should seek to broaden the scope of Schengen-relatedness in those fields which were covered by the Convention Implementing the Schengen Agreement, or which otherwise are closely connected to Schengen. Based on a political agreement to be found, a clarifying Council Decision could be proposed, together with an "omnibus proposal" declaring as Schengen-related those legal acts which would fall under the scope of this renewed understanding.

> The withdrawal of the UK offers a window of opportunity to sort out things now. It may be a good idea to have a calm look at issues now and agree on a renewed definition of the scope of the Schengen acquis, somehow like it was done with Council Decision 99/437/EC. Whatever approach will be chosen, the label of "Schengen" as a well-known brand should be maintained.

Chapter 6
Conclusions

6.1 Schengen: A Success Story with an Unconventional Birth

Schengen was launched, in the mid-1980s, as an intergovernmental project. The intergovernmental roots of Schengen can only be understood in a historical context: In the mid-1980s, a number of (continental) EC Member States were in principle open to abandon internal border control for the purpose of achieving the Single Market, but the UK preferred to keep sovereign border control and it rejected—under the unanimity requirement prevailing at that time on that issue—any attempt to abandon internal border control as an EC law measure. Those Member States which were willing to abandon internal border controls in an EC law context were therefore prevented from doing so. In the mid-1980s, EC law also did not yet provide for systems of enhanced cooperation between Member States within the EC law context. Such possibility, which allows a group of Member States to establish between themselves more far reaching cooperation within the framework of the Union, was only introduced by the Treaty of Amsterdam in 1999. Thus, in the 1980s, the only way in which the willing EC Member States could achieve the objective of abandoning internal border control, was to commit the "sin" of having recourse to intergovernmental cooperation. With the entry into force of the Amsterdam Treaty and its Schengen Protocol in 1999, Schengen was integrated into the framework of the EU as first project of "closer cooperation" formally authorized by the EU institutions.

The price which was paid for ending the first "sin" (the intergovernmental cooperation), was to commit another "sin", namely authorising, from 1999 onwards, a number of Members States (UK, Ireland, Denmark) and Schengen associated third countries (Iceland, Norway and later Switzerland and Liechtenstein) to participate (or not to participate) in Schengen related legal acts in accordance with their respective, legally complex, Protocols or Association agreements. This so called "variable geometry" arrangement resulted in high legal complexity, as described in detail in Chap. 4 of this guide.

© The Author(s), under exclusive license to Springer Nature Switzerland AG 2024
F. Lutz, *Practical Guide to Schengen Law*, SpringerBriefs in Law, https://doi.org/10.1007/978-3-031-56898-5_6

In spite of its complex genesis, Schengen turned out to be one of the biggest European success stories. "Schengen" has today become a well-known brand and established European identifier. It is important not to forget that the alleged "Schengen crisis", lamented frequently in recent years (Votoupalová, 2020, p. 414), affects primarily one (key) aspect of the Schengen acquis, namely the absence of—but potential need for—internal border control. Other components of Schengen law continue to operate smoothly, such as the common visa policy, the application of harmonized rules at external borders and the functioning of the Schengen Information System as the "crown jewel" (De Capitani, 2014, p. 104) of internal security.

6.2 Complexity Is Impacting Legal Certainty and Policy Making

The experiences with Schengen cooperation, over the last decades, teaches us that a geometry of closer cooperation has similarities with mathematic equations: In order to make closer cooperation work smoothly, ambiguity on the scope of closer cooperations needs to be avoided, precise and binding criteria for settling newly emerging questions need to be in place and clear criteria on decision-shaping and decision-making must be agreed upon in advance. These parameters then need to be stringently applied and any change to them should be agreed upon by all, and made transparent.

It was shown in Chap. 2 of this guide that the lack of mathematical precision in the Schengen Protocol as well as in Schengen Association Agreements that would have been necessary to clearly determine the substantive scope of Schengen law, as opposed to the "normal" EU Justice and Home Affairs rules which evolved in parallel, led to persistent legal debates, legal uncertainty, and differing approaches. A noteworthy illustration of this finding is the fact that the Schengen/non-Schengen nature of responsibility rules for asylum seekers (Dublin rules) are still an issue of legal debate 22 years after the integration of the Schengen acquis into the Framework of the EU. Mathematical precision was also absent and overruled by policy considerations, when determining the Schengen-relatedness of the new EU legal instruments in the field of police and judicial cooperation, adopted after 1999 (see above Sect. 3.2).

The resulting legal complexity has become more than just a technical problem. Legal certainty is undermined in multiple ways: by the need to draft two or sometimes three parallel proposals addressing different legal "audiences" to cover one and the same policy field; by the need to conclude parallel agreements to ensure Danish, Norwegian, Swiss, Icelandic and Liechtenstein participation in policy fields which were previously labelled as Schengen-related but are not considered Schengen related any more today (e.g. the Dublin rules); and by uncertainty on the continued applicability of provisions of the Convention Implementing the Schengen Agreement on police and judicial cooperation, resulting from the splitting of this policy field into Schengen related and non-Schengen-related parts. In the field of external relations, variable geometry created untold technical complications which made the Union's international life miserable (Kuijper, 2004, p. 626).

This legal complexity consumes time and administrative resources, and the related legal debates delay political decision-making. A telling example of the latter is the February 2021 40 pages Council Legal Service opinion on the "variable geometry" aspects of the Pact on Migration and Asylum (Council document 6357/21). Another example is the fact that—despite several efforts by the EU Publication Office—as at the date of publication of this guide, it had not been possible to produce a consolidated version of the currently applicable text of the Convention Implementing the Schengen Agreement. This fact can be explained by uncertainty as to which Articles have been repealed, replaced, superseded, or remained partially applicable (in relations between Member States and Schengen Associated States but not between Member States themselves). It means that law practitioners working with that instrument lack an appropriate tool to learn which provisions of it are still in force, and which are not.

Example of Legal Complexity

The recitals of the eu-Lisa Regulation (EU) 2018/1726 demonstrate, in an impressive way, the complexity which has been created, over the last two decades, by the co-existence of Schengen and non-Schengen-related acts in the field of Justice and Home Affairs. Recital 53 (on Ireland) is reproduced here, as an example:

(53) Insofar as its provisions relate to SIS II as governed by Decision 2007/533/JHA, Ireland could, in principle, take part in this Regulation, in accordance with Article 5(1) of Protocol No 19 and Article 6(2) of Council Decision 2002/192/EC. Insofar as its provisions relate to SIS II as governed by Regulation (EC) No 1987/2006 and to the VIS, to the EES and to ETIAS, this Regulation constitutes a development of the provisions of the Schengen acquis in which Ireland does not take part, in accordance with Decision 2002/192/EC; Ireland has not requested to take part in the adoption of this Regulation, in accordance with Article 4 of Protocol No 19. Ireland is therefore not taking part in the adoption of this Regulation and is not bound by it or subject to its application to the extent that its measures develop provisions of the Schengen acquis as they relate to SIS II as governed by Regulation (EC) No 1987/2006, to the VIS, to the EES and to ETIAS. Furthermore, insofar as its provisions relate to Eurodac and DubliNet, in accordance with Articles 1 and 2 and Article 4a(1) of Protocol No 21, Ireland is not taking part in the adoption of this Regulation and is not bound by it or subject to its application. Since it is not possible, under these circumstances, to ensure that this Regulation is applicable in its entirety to Ireland, as required by Article 288 TFEU, Ireland is not taking part in the adoption of this Regulation and is not

> bound by it or subject to its application, without prejudice to its rights under Protocols No 19 and No 21.
>
> Having read that recital one may assume that Ireland is not participating in that Regulation. But this impression is wrong: The recital only reflects the situation at the moment of the publication of that Regulation and it was superseded in 2019 by Council Decision 2019/1749 concerning the request of Ireland to take part in some of the provisions of the Schengen acquis relating to eu-LISA which authorised Irish participation Ireland in Regulation (EU) 2018/1726 to the extent that it relates to the operational management of the VIS, the parts of SIS in which Ireland does not take part and the EES and ETIAS.

The withdrawal of the United Kingdom from the EU already reduced—looked at from a "variable geometry" angle—the existing complexity, since it reduced the number of Member States benefitting from *a la carte* participation in the field of Justice and Home Affairs and Schengen. What could be done to further improve the situation?

6.3 Reducing Complexity by Adjusting the Scope of Schengen Law?

In principle, there are three options to respond to the complexity in Schengen law that could be realized without necessarily changing the Treaties and Protocols:

1. Agree on a *broader interpretation* of the scope of the Schengen acquis. This would imply a (re)labelling as Schengen-related of all (or some) legal acts which regulate subject matters covered by the scope of the 1990 Convention Implementing the Schengen Agreement. It could, for instance, affect measures in the field of police and judicial cooperation and responsibility for asylum seekers (Dublin) and bring those back within the formal scope of the Schengen acquis.
2. Agree on a *narrower interpretation* of the scope of the Schengen acquis. This would imply a (re)labelling as non-Schengen-related of all (or some) legal acts which are currently considered as Schengen-related and which currently co-exist with closely related non-Schengen measures. It could, for instance, affect measures in the field of police and judicial cooperation, irregular migration, drugs, firearms and data protection.
3. Continue with the *current middle-way* (historically grown, mixed approach).

Each of these three options has its pros and cons. Before arriving at any conclusion, the impact of these three options needs to be analysed rationally, looking at the effect it may have on each of the most involved States and the EU as a whole:

As regards *Denmark*, a broader approach would allow this State to participate, through its Schengen participation under Article 4 of the Denmark Protocol, in more EU legal acts. A narrower approach the contrary. Therefore, a broader interpretation of the scope of the Schengen acquis might be in the interest of Denmark, since it would allow Denmark to participate directly in more EU acts in the field of Justice and Home Affairs, rather than having to conclude separate bilateral agreements for participating in these, as is the practice today. In this context it must also be highlighted that the limited participation of Denmark is self-imposed and that Denmark may, at any time, avail itself of the options under either Article 7 or Article 8 of the Denmark Protocol (see Sect. 4.3 above) and participate more broadly in the EUs freedom, security and justice acquis.

As regards *Ireland*, a broader interpretation of the scope of the Schengen acquis might require this State to also broaden the scope of its Schengen participation in relation to certain non-border related Schengen issues, not yet covered by the partial Irish Schengen participation. A narrower approach and the resulting Irish non-participation in legal acts under its already authorized partial Schengen participation, could be easily compensated by Ireland by means of opt-ins under the UK/Ireland Protocol 21 (see Sect. 4.2 above), since for all non-Schengen related legal acts, that Protocol allows Ireland to selectively opt in or opt out. Therefore, there are arguments for assuming that Ireland could probably equally live with both a broader and a narrower interpretation of the scope of the Schengen acquis.

As regards the *Schengen Associated States (Norway, Iceland, Switzerland, Liechtenstein)*, a broader interpretation of the scope of the Schengen acquis would imply direct participation in more EU Justice and Home Affairs measures (such as for instance the European Arrest Warrant Framework Decision 2002/584/JHA, the Prüm II Framework Decision 2008/615/JHA or the Europol Regulation (EU) 2016/794) without EU membership, and it would simplify their participation in those measures, which currently often takes place under separate bilateral agreements or arrangements. A narrower approach would mean the contrary. The policy preferences of these States for either approach is likely to vary, depending on the national perception of whether direct participation in more EU Justice and Home Affairs measures is a good or a bad thing.

For the *European Union*, a broader approach would reflect the political narrative, already prevailing in Schengen-related policy documents (see, for instance, the Commissions 2024 State of Schengen report COM(2024)173), that the political "Schengen" is broader than the formally labelled Schengen acquis and that it already encompasses many of the measures adopted in the field of Justice and Home Affairs as "normal" EU law, such as the Prüm II police cooperation framework, the European Arrest Warrant, responsibility rules on asylum seekers (Dublin and Eurodac), Europol and others (the so called "*lost children of Schengen*" mentioned above in Sect. 2.6). However, the question arises, whether direct participation of States that are not EU members in these key Justice and Home Affairs instruments is politically desirable. On the one hand, direct participation of associated States in those measures may be seen as enhancing security in the EU. It would also make redundant the current practice of concluding separate bilateral agreements or arrangements to allow Norway, Iceland, Switzerland and Liechtenstein to participate in selected EU Justice and Home Affairs measures. On the other hand, there is the valid argument raised in research interviews (see above chapter; replies to question 5) that these measures require a degree of mutual trust which can only be present between Member States and not between Member States and associated States, and that associated States should become Member States if they want to benefit from full participation in EU Justice and Home Affairs measures.

6.4 Or Merging the Worlds of Schengen Law and Normal EU Law?

An alternative and more radical option, which would, however, require a change of the EU Treaties, would be to completely abandon the concept of Schengen acquis, and to treat, in the future, Schengen law just like normal Union law. Such an approach would probably have to go hand-in-hand with a special derogation for Ireland to maintain the Common Travel Area providing for free movement between the United Kingdom and Ireland (see above Sect. 4.2), and with a renewed legal frame for involving Schengen Associated States via an extended, European Economic Area (EEA)-like, arrangement. The Schengen Evaluation System could be replaced by a broader "Justice and Home Affairs evaluation mechanism", for which a legal basis would already exist in accordance with Article 70 TFEU.

This radical approach would be consistent with the initial idea of Schengen to serve as a test-laboratory for European integration and the objective, present from the outset in the Schengen Agreements (Articles 134 and 142 of the Convention Implementing the Schengen Agreement—see above, Sect. 1.2), that Schengen rules should—in the long term—gradually be accepted by all Member States in the form of EC/EU law. This "dynamic" process had been blocked, since 1999, due to the Schengen Protocol and the Denmark Protocol as well as the Schengen Association Agreements, which all foresaw a "freezing" of the subject matters considered as Schengen-related as they were in 1999 or upon conclusion of the Association Agreements (see above Sect. 2.6.1). This static "freezing" of Schengen-related and non-Schengen related subject matters by the Amsterdam Treaty resulted in the perpetuation of two parallel worlds: the world of Schengen law and the world of normal EU law and as a consequence, since 1999, the long-term objective of fully merging Schengen law with "normal" EU law has been put on hold for an indefinite period. Should this separation of two parallel words, dealing with closely related issues, be maintained forever?

Support for the radical option of fully merging Schengen with Union law, can also be found in the argument that the area of freedom, security and justice envisaged by Part Three, Title V TFEU is built on the same principles of a balance of benefits and burdens and of mutual trust as the original Schengen Treaties. A valid case can be made that, when politicians refer today to the need to 'reset' or 'complete' Schengen, they are in fact referring to the need to revise the whole area of freedom, security and justice, as Schengen has in effect been turned into and absorbed by that area. From a practical and political perspective, Schengen and the area of freedom, security and justice may be considered as having become one and the same (Ueberecken, 2019, p. 3).

6.5 What Next?

Currently, the question of Schengen-relatedness is always only discussed in the context of one or some specific legislative proposals. This piecemeal approach doesn't contribute to coherent and sustainable solutions. It may therefore be a good idea to carry out a broader horizontal assessment of the concept of Schengen-relatedness. The withdrawal of the United Kingdom offers a window of opportunity to do so now, and to have a fresh look at the subject matters to be considered as Schengen-related. Such Schengen reflections could be carried out jointly by Council, Commission, European Parliament and the most affected States (i.e., Denmark, Ireland, and Schengen Associated States) in a "friends of Schengen Group". Based on a political agreement, prepared by that group, on the line to follow, a clarifying Council Decision might be proposed, together with an "omnibus proposal", declaring as Schengen-related (or not-Schengen-related) those legal acts or groups of legal acts which would fall under the scope of a renewed understanding of Schengen-relatedness.

As a complement, and in addition, a more far-reaching long-term perspective involving a change of the Treaties and Protocols, aimed at merging the world of Schengen law with the world of normal EU law could also be developed and recommended. Such solution is probably—like any Treaty change—difficult to realise. But there would nevertheless be added value of developing and putting on paper a clear concept on the way to move ahead. This concept could then be used in the future, once a window of opportunity for changing the Treaties might open.

Since the notion of "Schengen" is a well-known brand and clearly more popular than any technical acronym, like JHA (Justice and Home Affairs) or AFSJ (area of freedom, security, and justice), the label of "Schengen", as a well-established European identifier, should be maintained, whatever solution will be agreed upon.

References

De Capitani, E. (2014). The Schengen system after Lisbon: From cooperation to integration. *ERA Forum, 15*(1), 101–118.
Kuijper, P. J. (2004). Evolution of the third pillar from Maastricht to the European Constitution: Institutional aspects. *Common Market Law Review, 41*, 609.
Ueberecken, R. (2019). *Schengen reloaded.* Centre for European Reform.
Votoupalová, M. (2020). Schengen cooperation: What scholars make of it. *Journal of Borderlands Studies, 35*(3), 403–423.

Consolidated Text of the 1990 Convention Implementing the Schengen Agreement (CISA)

Disclaimer:
- This is an informal and non-authentic consolidation. In case of doubt, the legal texts published in the Official Journal and EUR-Lex should be consulted and prevail.

Remarks:
- This version reflects the situation as on 1 May 2024.

- To make this annex fit into the format of SpringerBriefs the text of some replaced, deleted or obsolete provisions was deleted and marked with (…). The full text of these Articles can be retrieved in the Official Journal L 239 of 22 September 2000, p. 19-82.

- Provisions for which, according to Council Decision 1999/435/EC, it was not considered necessary to determine a legal basis and which were therefore printed in italics in the publication of the Schengen acquis in Official Journal L 239 of 22 September 2000, *are printed in italics.*

- Provisions which are not yet applicable are placed in brackets and explanation is provided in footnotes. (This is only relevant in the context of Articles 18 and 20 CISA.)

- Repealed, replaced, deleted or obsolete provisions are printed in normal typesetting and not in bold. **In those cases, in which the legal status of a provision is not clear, explanations are provided in the footnotes.**

- Some provisions have been superseded, or replaced by EC/EU law as far as relations between Member States are concerned, but remain in force in relations with Schengen associated States. This is explained in the relevant footnotes.

TITLE I
DEFINITIONS
Article 1
For the purposes of this Convention:

internal borders: shall mean the common land borders of the Contracting Parties, their airports for internal flights and their sea ports for regular ferry connections exclusively from or to other ports within the territories of the Contracting Parties and not calling at any ports outside those territories;

external borders: shall mean the Contracting Parties' land and sea borders and their airports and sea ports, provided that they are not internal borders;

internal flight: shall mean any flight exclusively to or from the territories of the Contracting Parties and not landing in the territory of a third State;[1]

third State: shall mean any State other than the Contracting Parties;[2]

alien: shall mean any person other than a national of a Member State of the European Communities;[3]

alien for whom an alert has been issued for the purposes of refusing entry: shall mean an alien for whom an alert has been introduced into the Schengen Information System in accordance with Article 96 with a view to that person being refused entry;[4]

border crossing point: shall mean any crossing point authorised by the competent authorities for crossing external borders;

border check: shall mean a check carried out at a border in response exclusively to an intention to cross that border, regardless of any other consideration;[5]

carrier: shall mean any natural or legal person whose occupation it is to provide passenger transport by air, sea or land;[6]

residence permit: shall mean an authorisation of whatever type issued by a Contracting Party which grants right of residence within its territory. This definition shall not include temporary permission to reside in the territory of a

---

[1] These three definitions were never formally repealed but can be considered as superseded (*lex posterior* rule) by the definitions contained in Regulation (EC) No 562/2006 (Schengen Borders Code), which replaced Articles 2-8 CISA.

[2] This definition (also) relates to a provision of CISA that is still in force (Article 26). It is essentially similar to the definition of "third country" used in more recent Schengen legal acts.

[3] This definition (also) relates to provisions of CISA that are still in force (Articles 18–22, 26, 40, 45). It is essentially similar to the definition of "third-country national" used in more recent Schengen legal acts.

[4] This definition was never formally repealed. It is used only once in the context of Article 25 CISA and can be considered as obsolete since the repeal of Article 25 CISA by Article 64 of the SIS (border) Regulation (EU) 2018/1861.

[5] These two definitions were never formally repealed but can be considered as superseded (*lex posterior* rule) by the definitions contained in Regulation (EC) No 562/2006 (Schengen Borders Code), which replaced Articles 2-8 CISA.

[6] This definition relates to a provision of CISA that is still in force (Article 26). It is essentially similar (but not the same) as the definition of "carrier" in Regulation (EC) No 562/2006 (Schengen Borders Code).

Contracting Party for the purposes of processing an application for asylum or a residence permit;[7]

application for asylum: shall mean any application submitted in writing, orally or otherwise by an alien at an external border or within the territory of a Contracting Party with a view to obtaining recognition as a refugee in accordance with the Geneva Convention relating to the Status of Refugees of 28 July 1951, as amended by the New York Protocol of 31 January 1967, and as such obtaining the right of residence;

asylum seeker: shall mean any alien who has lodged an application for asylum within the meaning of this Convention and in respect of which a final decision has not yet been taken;

processing applications for asylum: shall mean all the procedures for examining and taking a decision on applications for asylum, including measures taken under a final decision thereon, with the exception of the determination of the Contracting Party responsible for processing applications for asylum pursuant to this Convention.[8]

TITLE II
ABOLITION OF CHECKS AT INTERNAL BORDERS AND MOVEMENT OF PERSONS

CHAPTER 1
CROSSING INTERNAL BORDERS
(…)[9]

CHAPTER 2
CROSSING EXTERNAL BORDERS
(…)[10]

CHAPTER 3
VISAS

Section 1
Short-stay visas
(…)[11]

---

[7] This definition is used in nine Articles of CISA, of which seven have been replaced/repealed (Articles 5, 23, 25, 30, 33, 38 and 92) and two are still in force (Articles 18 and 21). It is not clear whether this definition can be considered as obsolete. On the one hand, it can be argued that it was superseded (*lex posterior* rule) by the more restrictive definition of "residence permit" contained in Regulation (EC) No 562/2006 (Schengen Borders Code) that should be applied horizontally. On the other hand, it can be argued that it remains applicable for the specific purposes of Articles 18 and 21 CISA.

[8] These three asylum related definitions were formally repealed, by Article 1 of the 1994 "Bonn Protocol" Sch/Com-ex (94)3) (published in BGBl 1995 II, 739), which replaced Articles 28–38 CISA and the three asylum related definitions in Article 1 CISA.

[9] Repealed and replaced by Regulation (EC) No 562/2006 (Schengen Borders Code).

[10] Repealed and replaced by Regulation (EC) No 562/2006 (Schengen Borders Code).

[11] Repealed and replaced by Regulation (EC) No 810/2009 (Visa Code).

Section 2
Long-stay visas
Article 18[12]

1. Visas for stays exceeding 90 days (long-stay visas) shall be national visas issued by one of the Member States in accordance with its national law or Union law. Such visas shall be issued in the uniform format for visas as set out in Council Regulation (EC) No 1683/95 with the heading specifying the type of visa with the letter "D". They shall be filled out in accordance with the relevant provisions of Annex VII to Regulation (EC) No 810/2009 of the European Parliament and of the Council of 13 July 2009 establishing a Community Code on Visas (Visa Code).

(1. Visas for stays exceeding 90 days (long-stay visas) shall be national visas issued by one of the Member States in accordance with its national law or with Union law. Such visas shall be issued in digital format in accordance with Article 1 of Council Regulation (EC) No 1683/95, with the type of visa being indicated with the letter "D". Long-stay visas issued in digital format shall be filled out in accordance with the relevant provisions of the Commission implementing act setting out the rules for filling in the data fields of the visa, adopted in accordance with Article 27(1) of Regulation (EC) No 810/2009 of the European Parliament and of the Council.

1a. Long-stay visas issued in digital format shall be communicated to applicants by electronic means by the competent authorities of the issuing Member State.)[13]

2. Long-stay visas shall have a period of validity of no more than one year. If a Member State allows an alien to stay for more than one year, the long-stay visa shall be replaced before the expiry of its period of validity by a residence permit.

CHAPTER 4
CONDITIONS GOVERNING THE MOVEMENT OF ALIENS
Article 19

1. Aliens who hold uniform visas and who have legally entered the territory of a Contracting Party may move freely within the territories of all the Contracting Parties during the period of validity of their visas, provided that they fulfil the entry conditions referred to in Article 5(1)(a), (c), (d) and (e)[14].

---

[12] Article 18 was modified several times. The currently applicable text is based on Regulation (EU) 265/2010 and Regulation (EU) 610/2013 (the latter changed horizontally the previously used term "three months" to "90 days" in a number of Schengen related legal acts).

[13] Paragraph 1 was changed and paragraph 1a added by Regulation (EU) 2023/2667 regarding the digitalisation of the visa procedure. **Not yet applicable. Will become applicable from the date set by the Commission in accordance with Article 7(1) of Regulation (EU) 2023/2667 (start of operation of the EU Visa Application Platform).**

[14] In accordance with Article 39(3) Schengen Borders Code (version predating the codification), these references shall be construed as reference to Article 6(1) SBC.

2. *Pending the introduction of a uniform visa, aliens who hold visas issued by one of the Contracting Parties and who have legally entered the territory of one Contracting Party may move freely within the territories of all the Contracting Parties during the period of validity of their visas up to a maximum of three months from the date of first entry, provided that they fulfil the entry conditions referred to in Article 5(1)(a), (c), (d) and (e).*[15]

3. **Paragraphs 1 and 2 shall not apply to visas whose validity is subject to territorial limitation in accordance with Chapter 3 of this Title.**

4. **This Article shall apply without prejudice to Article 22.**

Article 20

1. **Aliens not subject to a visa requirement may move freely within the territories of the Contracting Parties for a maximum period of 90 days in any 180-day period**[16]**, provided that they fulfil the entry conditions referred to in Article 5(1)(a), (c), (d) and (e)**[17]**.**

2. **Paragraph 1 shall not affect each Contracting Party's right to extend beyond 90 days**[18] **an alien's stay in its territory in exceptional circumstances or in accordance with a bilateral agreement concluded before the entry into force of this Convention (and notified to the Commission in accordance with paragraph 2d.)**[19]**;**

(2a. **The stay of an alien on the territory of a Contracting Party may be extended in accordance with a bilateral agreement pursuant to point (b) of paragraph 2, upon request of the alien, and lodged with the competent authorities of that Contracting Party on entry or during the stay of the alien at the latest on the last working day of his or her 90-day stay in any 180-day period.**

Where the alien has not lodged a request during the 90-day stay in any 180-day period, his or her stay may be extended pursuant to a bilateral agreement concluded by a Contracting Party and his or her stay beyond the 90-day stay in any 180-day period preceding that extension may be presumed lawful by the competent authorities of that Contracting Party, provided that that alien presents credible evidence which proves that during that time he or she stayed only on the territory of that Contracting Party.

---

[15] According to Council Decision 1999/435/EC, it was not considered necessary to determine a legal basis for Article 19(2) and it was therefore printed in italics in the publication of the Schengen acquis in Official Journal L 239 of 22 September 2000. It had become obsolete due to the adoption of Regulation (EC) No 1683/95 laying down a uniform format for visa.

[16] Modified by Regulation (EU) 610/2013, which changed horizontally the previously used term "three months during six months" to "90 days within 180 days" in a number of Schengen related legal acts.

[17] In accordance with Article 39(3) Schengen Borders Code (version predating the codification), these references shall be construed as reference to Article 6(1) SBC.

[18] Modified by Regulation (EU) 610/2013.

[19] Last part of para 2 was inserted by Article 60 of the EES Regulation (EU) 2017/2226. **Not yet applicable. Will become applicable with start of operation of the Entry-Exit System (EES).**

2b. Where the stay is extended pursuant to paragraph 2 of this Article, the competent authorities of that Contracting Party shall enter the data related to the extension in the latest relevant entry/exit record linked to the alien's individual file contained in the Entry/Exit System established by Regulation (EU) 2017/2226 of the European Parliament and of the Council. Such data shall be entered in accordance with Article 19 of that Regulation.

2c. Where the stay is extended pursuant to paragraph 2, the alien concerned shall be authorised to stay only on the territory of that Contracting Party and exit at the external borders of that Contracting Party.

The competent authority which extended the stay shall inform the alien concerned that the extension of stay authorises the alien concerned to stay only on the territory of that Contracting Party and that he or she is to exit at the external borders of that Contracting party.

2d. By 30 March 2018, the Contracting Parties shall notify the text of their relevant applicable bilateral agreements as referred to in point (b) of paragraph 2 to the Commission. If a Contracting Party ceases to apply any of those bilateral agreements, it shall notify the Commission thereof. The Commission shall publish information about such bilateral agreements in the Official Journal of the European Union, including at least the Member States and third countries concerned, the rights derived for aliens from those bilateral agreements, as well as any changes thereto.)[20]

3. This Article shall apply without prejudice to Article 22.

Article 21[21]

1. Aliens who hold valid residence permits issued by one of the Member States may, on the basis of that permit and a valid travel document, move freely for up 90 days in any 180-day period within the territories of the other Member States, provided that they fulfil the entry conditions referred to in Article 5(1) (a), (c) and (e) of Regulation (EC) No 562/2006 of the European Parliament and of the Council of 15 March 2006 establishing a Community Code on the rules governing the movement of persons across borders (Schengen Borders Code) and are not on the national list of alerts of the Member State concerned.

2. Paragraph 1 shall also apply to aliens who hold provisional residence permits issued by one of the Contracting Parties and travel documents issued by that Contracting Party.

2a. The right of free movement laid down in paragraph 1 shall also apply to aliens who hold a valid long-stay visa issued by one of the Member States as provided for in Article 18.

---

[20] Inserted by Article 60 of the EES Regulation (EU) 2017/2226. **Not yet applicable. Will become applicable with start of operation of the Entry-Exit System (EES).**

[21] As modified by Regulations (EU) 265/2010 and 610/2013.

3. The Contracting Parties shall send the Executive Committee a list of the documents that they issue as valid travel documents, residence permits or provisional residence permits within the meaning of this Article.[22]

4. This Article shall apply without prejudice to Article 22.

Article 22[23]

Aliens who have legally entered the territory of one of the Contracting Parties may be obliged to report, in accordance with the conditions laid down by each Contracting Party, to the competent authorities of the Contracting Party whose territory they enter. Such aliens shall report either on entry or within three working days of entry, at the discretion of the Contracting Party whose territory they enter.

Article 23 and 24

(…)[24]

CHAPTER 5

RESIDENCE PERMITS AND ALERTS FOR THE PURPOSES OF REFUSING ENTRY

Article 25

(…)[25]

CHAPTER 6

ACCOMPANYING MEASURES

Article 26[26]

1. The Contracting Parties undertake, subject to the obligations resulting from their accession to the Geneva Convention relating to the Status of Refugees of 28 July 1951, as amended by the New York Protocol of 31 January 1967, to incorporate the following rules into their national law:

(a) If aliens are refused entry into the territory of one of the Contracting Parties, the carrier which brought them to the external border by air, sea or land shall be obliged immediately to assume responsibility for them again. At the request of the border surveillance authorities the carrier shall be obliged to return the aliens to the third State from which they were transported or to the third State which issued the travel document on which they travelled or to any other third State to which they are certain to be admitted.

(b) The carrier shall be obliged to take all the necessary measures to ensure that an alien carried by air or sea is in possession of the travel documents required for entry into the territories of the Contracting Parties.

2. The Contracting Parties undertake, subject to the obligations resulting from their accession to the Geneva Convention relating to the Status of Refugees

---

[22] Deleted by Regulation (EU) 610/2013.

[23] As modified by Regulation (EU) 610/2013.

[24] Articles 23 and 24 were repealed and replaced by the Return Directive 2008/115/EC.

[25] Article 25 had been amended by Regulation (EU) 265/2010 and was subsequently repealed by Article 64 of the SIS (border) Regulation (EU) 2018/1861.

[26] The provisions of Article 26 are still in force. They were, however, supplemented by the provisions of Directive 2001/51/EC.

of 28 July 1951, as amended by the New York Protocol of 31 January 1967, and in accordance with their constitutional law, to impose penalties on carriers which transport aliens who do not possess the necessary travel documents by air or sea from a Third State to their territories.

3. Paragraphs 1(b) and 2 shall also apply to international carriers transporting groups overland by coach, with the exception of border traffic.

Article 27

(…)[27]

CHAPTER 7
RESPONSIBILITY FOR PROCESSING APPLICATIONS FOR ASYLUM

(…)[28]

TITLE III
POLICE AND SECURITY
CHAPTER 1
POLICE COOPERATION

Article 39[29]

1. The Contracting Parties undertake to ensure that their police authorities shall, in compliance with national law and within the scope of their powers, assist each other for the purposes of preventing and detecting criminal offences, in so far as national law does not stipulate that the request has to be made and channelled via the judicial authorities and provided that the request or the implementation thereof does not involve the application of measures of constraint by the requested Contracting Party. Where the requested police authorities do not have the power to deal with a request, they shall forward it to the competent authorities.

---

[27] Article 27(1) was repealed by Directive 2002/90/EC. Article 27(2) and (3) were repealed by Framework Decision 2002/946/JHA.

[28] Footnote 2 of Council Decision 1999/435/EC sets out that this chapter is "*Replaced by the Convention, signed in Dublin on 15 June 1990, determining the State responsible for examining applications for asylum lodged in one of the Member States of the European Communities (OJ C 254, 19.8.1997, p. 1)*". This replacement, provided for in the 1994 "Bonn Protocol" (Sch/Com-ex (94)3) (published in BGBl 1995 II, 739) took place in 1997.

[29] Articles 39 and 46 CISA contain rules on information exchange between police authorities, which were further developed and partly replaced by Framework Decision 2006/960/JHA on simplifying the exchange of information and intelligence between law enforcement authorities of the Member States of the European Union ("Swedish Initiative" - labelled as Schengen related), in as far as they relate to exchange of information and intelligence for the purpose of conducting criminal investigations or criminal intelligence operations as provided for by that Framework Decision. From 12 December 2024, the parts of Articles 39 and 46 of the Convention implementing the Schengen Agreement that have not been replaced by Framework Decision 2006/960/JHA are **replaced** by Directive (EU) 2023/977 on the exchange of information between the law enforcement authorities of Member States and repealing Council Framework Decision 2006/960/JHA, **in so far as those Articles relate to the exchange of information falling within the scope of that Directive**. Article 39 continues to be applicable to other forms of police cooperation falling outside the scope of that Directive.

2. Written information provided by the requested Contracting Party under paragraph 1 may not be used by the requesting Contracting Party as evidence of the offence charged other than with the consent of the competent judicial authorities of the requested Contracting Party.

3. Requests for assistance referred to in paragraph 1 and the replies to such requests may be exchanged between the central bodies responsible in each Contracting Party for international police cooperation. Where the request cannot be made in good time using the above procedure, the police authorities of the requesting Contracting Party may address it directly to the competent authorities of the requested Party, which may reply directly. In such cases, the requesting police authority shall at the earliest opportunity inform the central body responsible for international police cooperation in the requested Contracting Party of its direct request.

4. In border areas, cooperation may be covered by arrangements between the competent Ministers of the Contracting Parties.

5. The provisions of this Article shall not preclude more detailed present or future bilateral agreements between Contracting Parties with a common border. The Contracting Parties shall inform each other of such agreements.

Article 40

1. Officers of one of the Member States who are keeping a person under surveillance in their country as part of a criminal investigation into an extraditable criminal offence because he is suspected of involvement in an extraditable criminal offence or, as a necessary part of a criminal investigation, because there is serious reason to believe that he can assist in identifying or tracing such a person, shall be authorised to continue their surveillance in the territory of another Member State where the latter has authorised cross-border surveillance in response to a request for assistance made in advance with supporting reasons. Conditions may be attached to the authorisation.[30]

2. Where, for particularly urgent reasons, prior authorisation cannot be requested from the other Contracting Party, the officers carrying out the surveillance shall be authorised to continue beyond the border the surveillance of a person presumed to have committed criminal offences listed in paragraph 7, provided that the following conditions are met:

(a) the authority of the Contracting Party designated under paragraph 5, in whose territory the surveillance is to be continued, must be notified immediately, during the surveillance, that the border has been crossed;

(b) a request for assistance submitted in accordance with paragraph 1 and outlining the grounds for crossing the border without prior authorisation shall be submitted immediately.

Surveillance shall cease as soon as the Contracting Party in whose territory it is taking place so requests, following the notification referred to in (a) or the

---

[30] Text of para 1 as amended by Council Decision 2003/725/JHA.

request referred to in (b) or, where authorisation has not been obtained, five hours after the border was crossed.

3. The surveillance referred to in paragraphs 1 and 2 shall be carried out only under the following general conditions:

(a) The officers carrying out the surveillance must comply with the provisions of this Article and with the law of the Contracting Party in whose territory they are operating; they must obey the instructions of the competent local authorities.

(b) Except in the situations outlined in paragraph 2, the officers shall, during the surveillance, carry a document certifying that authorisation has been granted.

(c) The officers carrying out the surveillance must at all times be able to prove that they are acting in an official capacity.

(d) The officers carrying out the surveillance may carry their service weapons during the surveillance save where specifically otherwise decided by the requested Party; their use shall be prohibited save in cases of legitimate self-defence.

(e) Entry into private homes and places not accessible to the public shall be prohibited.

(f) The officers carrying out the surveillance may neither challenge nor arrest the person under surveillance.

(g) All operations shall be the subject of a report to the authorities of the Contracting Party in whose territory they took place; the officers carrying out the surveillance may be required to appear in person.

(h) The authorities of the Contracting Party from which the surveillance officers have come shall, when requested by the authorities of the Contracting Party in whose territory the surveillance took place, assist the enquiry subsequent to the operation in which they took part, including judicial proceedings.

4. The officers referred to in paragraphs 1 and 2 shall be[31]:

- as regards the Kingdom of Belgium: members of the "police judiciaire près les Parquets" (Criminal Police attached to the Public Prosecutor's Office), the "gendarmerie" and the "police communale" (municipal police), as well as customs officers, under the conditions laid down in appropriate bilateral agreements referred to in paragraph 6, with respect to their powers regarding illicit trafficking in narcotic drugs and psychotropic substances, trafficking in arms and explosives, and the illicit transportation of toxic and hazardous waste;

---

[31] To be read together with the amendments pursuant to the simplified procedure established by Council Decision 2000/586/JHA, establishing a procedure for amending Articles 40(4) and (5), 41(7) and 65(2) of CISA for providing references to 'officers', 'authorities' and 'competent Ministries' to the other Schengen States. This information is available in consolidated form in the Manual on cross border operations (Council document 13887/20) and its National Factsheets (Council document 13920/20).

- as regards the Federal Republic of Germany: officers of the "Polizeien des Bundes und der Länder" (Federal Police and Federal State Police), as well as, with respect only to illicit trafficking in narcotic drugs and psychotropic substances and arms trafficking, officers of the "Zollfahndungsdienst" (customs investigation service) in their capacity as auxiliary officers of the Public Prosecutor's Office;

- as regards the French Republic: criminal police officers of the national police and national "gendarmerie", as well as customs officers, under the conditions laid down in appropriate bilateral agreements referred to in paragraph 6, with respect to their powers regarding illicit trafficking in narcotic drugs and psychotropic substances, trafficking in arms and explosives, and the illicit transportation of toxic and hazardous waste;

- as regards the Grand Duchy of Luxembourg: officers of the "gendarmerie" and the police, as well as customs officers, under the conditions laid down in appropriate bilateral agreements referred to in paragraph 6, with respect to their powers regarding illicit trafficking in narcotic drugs and psychotropic substances, trafficking in arms and explosives, and the illicit transportation of toxic and hazardous waste;

- as regards the Kingdom of the Netherlands: officers of the "Rijkspolitie" (national police) and the "Gemeentepolitie" (municipal police), as well as, under the conditions laid down in appropriate bilateral agreements referred to in paragraph 6, with respect to their powers regarding illicit trafficking in narcotic drugs and psychotropic substances, trafficking in arms and explosives and the illicit transportation of toxic and hazardous waste, officers of the tax inspection and investigation authorities responsible for import and excise duties.

5. The authority referred to in paragraphs 1 and 2 shall be[32]:

- as regards the Kingdom of Belgium: the "Commissariat général de la Police judiciaire" (Criminal Investigation Department),

- as regards the Federal Republic of Germany: the "Bundeskriminalamt" (Federal Crime Office),

- as regards the French Republic: the "Direction centrale de la Police judiciaire" (Central Headquarters of the Criminal Police),

- as regards the Grand Duchy of Luxembourg: the "Procureur général d'Etat" (Principal State Prosecutor),

- as regards the Kingdom of the Netherlands: the "Landelijk Officier van Justitie" (National Public Prosecutor) responsible for cross-border surveillance.

6. The Contracting Parties may, at bilateral level, extend the scope of this Article and adopt additional measures in application thereof.

---

[32] See above FN on Article 40(4).

7. The surveillance referred to in paragraph 2 may only be carried out where one of the following criminal offences is involved:
- murder,
- manslaughter,
- a serious offence of a sexual nature,
- arson,
- counterfeiting and forgery of means of payment,
- aggravated burglary and robbery and receiving stolen goods,
- extortion,
- kidnapping and hostage taking,
- trafficking in human beings,
- illicit trafficking in narcotic drugs and psychotropic substances,
- breach of the laws on arms and explosives,
- wilful damage through the use of explosives,
- illicit transportation of toxic and hazardous waste
- serious fraud;
- smuggling of aliens;
- money laundering;
- illicit trafficking in nuclear and radioactive substances;
- participation in a criminal organisation as referred to in Council Joint Action 98/733/JHA of 21 December 1998 on making it a criminal offence to participate in a criminal organisation in the Member States of the European Union;
- terrorist offences as referred to in Council Framework Decision 2002/475/JHA of 13 June 2002 on combating terrorism.[33]

Article 41

1. Officers of one of the Contracting Parties who are pursuing in their country an individual caught in the act of committing or of participating in one of the offences referred to in paragraph 4 shall be authorised to continue pursuit in the territory of another Contracting Party without the latter's prior authorisation where, given the particular urgency of the situation, it is not possible to notify the competent authorities of the other Contracting Party by one of the means provided for in Article 44 prior to entry into that territory or where these authorities are unable to reach the scene in time to take over the pursuit.

The same shall apply where the person being pursued has escaped from provisional custody or while serving a sentence involving deprivation of liberty.

The pursuing officers shall, not later than when they cross the border, contact the competent authorities of the Contracting Party in whose territory the hot pursuit is to take place. The hot pursuit will cease as soon as the Contracting Party in whose territory the pursuit is taking place so requests. At the request of the pursuing officers, the competent local authorities shall challenge the pursued person in order to establish the person's identity or to make an arrest.

---

[33] Consolidated text of para 7 as amended by Council Decision 2003/725/JHA.

2. Hot pursuit shall be carried out in accordance with one of the following procedures, defined by the declaration laid down in paragraph 9:

(a) The pursuing officers shall not have the right to apprehend the pursued person;

(b) If no request to cease the hot pursuit is made and if the competent local authorities are unable to intervene quickly enough, the pursuing officers may detain the person pursued until the officers of the Contracting Party in whose territory the pursuit is taking place, who must be informed immediately, are able to establish the person's identity or make an arrest.

3. Hot pursuit shall be carried out in accordance with paragraphs 1 and 2 and in one of the following ways as defined by the declaration provided for in paragraph 9:

(a) in an area or during a period as from the crossing of the border, to be established in the declaration;

(b) without limit in space or time.

4. In the declaration referred to in paragraph 9, the Contracting Parties shall define the offences referred to in paragraph 1 in accordance with one of the following procedures:

(a) The following criminal offences:
- murder,
- manslaughter,
- rape,
- arson,
- forgery of money,
- aggravated burglary and robbery and receiving stolen goods,
- extortion,
- kidnapping and hostage taking,
- trafficking in human beings,
- illicit trafficking in narcotic drugs and psychotropic substances,
- breach of the laws on arms and explosives,
- wilful damage through the use of explosives,
- illicit transportation of toxic and hazardous waste,
- failure to stop and give particulars after an accident which has resulted in death or serious injury.

(b) Extraditable offences.

5. Hot pursuit shall be carried out only under the following general conditions:

(a) The pursuing officers must comply with the provisions of this Article and with the law of the Contracting Party in whose territory they are operating; they must obey the instructions issued by the competent local authorities.

(b) Pursuit shall be solely over land borders.

(c) Entry into private homes and places not accessible to the public shall be prohibited.

(d) The pursuing officers shall be easily identifiable, either by their uniform, by means of an armband or by accessories fitted to their vehicles; the use of civilian clothes combined with the use of unmarked vehicles without the aforementioned identification is prohibited; the pursuing officers must at all times be able to prove that they are acting in an official capacity.

(e) The pursuing officers may carry their service weapons; their use shall be prohibited save in cases of legitimate self-defence.

(f) Once the pursued person has been apprehended as provided for in paragraph 2(b), for the purpose of being brought before the competent local authorities that person may only be subjected to a security search; handcuffs may be used during the transfer; objects carried by the pursued person may be seized.

(g) After each operation referred to in paragraphs 1, 2 and 3, the pursuing officers shall appear before the competent local authorities of the Contracting Party in whose territory they were operating and shall report on their mission; at the request of those authorities, they shall remain at their disposal until the circumstances surrounding their action have been sufficiently clarified; this condition shall apply even where the hot pursuit has not resulted in the arrest of the person pursued.

(h) The authorities of the Contracting Party from which the pursuing officers have come shall, when requested by the authorities of the Contracting Party in whose territory the hot pursuit took place, assist the enquiry subsequent to the operation in which they took part, including judicial proceedings.

6. A person who, following the action provided for in paragraph 2, has been arrested by the competent local authorities may, whatever that person's nationality, be held for questioning. The relevant rules of national law shall apply mutatis mutandis.

If the person is not a national of the Contracting Party in whose territory the person was arrested, that person shall be released no later than six hours after the arrest was made, not including the hours between midnight and 9.00 a.m., unless the competent local authorities have previously received a request for that person's provisional arrest for the purposes of extradition in any form whatsoever.

7. The officers referred to in the previous paragraphs shall be[34]:

- as regards the Kingdom of Belgium: members of the "police judiciaire près les Parquets" (Criminal Police attached to the Public Prosecutor's Office), the "gendarmerie" and the "police communale" (municipal police), as well as customs officers, under the conditions laid down in appropriate bilateral agreements referred to in paragraph 10, with respect to their powers regarding illicit trafficking in narcotic drugs and psychotropic substances, trafficking in arms and explosives, and the illicit transportation of toxic and hazardous waste;

---

[34] See above FN on Article 40(4).

- as regards the Federal Republic of Germany: officers of the "Polizeien des Bundes und der Länder" (Federal and Federal State Police), as well as, with respect only to illegal trafficking in narcotic drugs and psychotropic substances and arms trafficking, officers of the "Zollfahndungsdienst" (customs investigation service) in their capacity as auxiliary officers of the Public Prosecutor's Office;
- as regards the French Republic: criminal police officers of the national police and national "gendarmerie", as well as customs officers, under the conditions laid down in the appropriate bilateral agreements referred to in paragraph 10, with respect to their powers regarding illicit trafficking in narcotic drugs and psychotropic substances, trafficking in arms and explosives, and the illicit transportation of toxic and hazardous waste;
- as regards the Grand Duchy of Luxembourg: officers of the "gendarmerie" and the police, as well as customs officers, under the conditions laid down in the appropriate bilateral agreements referred to in paragraph 10, with respect to their powers regarding illicit trafficking in narcotic drugs and psychotropic substances, trafficking in arms and explosives, and the illicit transportation of toxic and hazardous waste:
- as regards the Kingdom of the Netherlands: officers of the "Rijkspolitie" (national police) and the "Gemeentepolitie" (municipal police) as well as, under the conditions laid down in the appropriate bilateral agreements referred to in paragraph 10, with respect to their powers regarding the illicit trafficking in narcotic drugs and psychotropic substances, trafficking in arms and explosives and the illicit transportation of toxic and hazardous waste, officers of the tax inspection and investigation authorities responsible for import and excise duties.

8. For the Contracting Parties concerned this Article shall apply without prejudice to Article 27 of the Benelux Treaty concerning Extradition and Mutual Assistance in Criminal Matters of 27 June 1962, as amended by the Protocol of 11 May 1974.

9. At the time of signing this Convention, each Contracting Party shall make a declaration in which it shall define for each of the Contracting Parties with which it has a common border, on the basis of paragraphs 2, 3 and 4, the procedures for carrying out a hot pursuit in its territory.

A Contracting Party may at any time replace its declaration by another declaration provided the latter does not restrict the scope of the former.

Each declaration shall be made after consultation with each of the Contracting Parties concerned and with a view to obtaining equivalent arrangements on both sides of internal borders.

10. The Contracting Parties may, on a bilateral basis, extend the scope of paragraph 1 and adopt additional provisions in implementation of this Article.

Article 42

During the operations referred to in Articles 40 and 41, officers operating in the territory of another Contracting Party shall be regarded as officers of that Party with respect to offences committed against them or by them.

Article 43

1. Where, in accordance with Articles 40 and 41 of this Convention, officers of a Contracting Party are operating in the territory of another Contracting Party, the first Contracting Party shall be liable for any damage caused by them during their operations, in accordance with the law of the Contracting Party in whose territory they are operating.

2. The Contracting Party in whose territory the damage referred to in paragraph 1 was caused shall make good such damage under the conditions applicable to damage caused by its own officers.

3. The Contracting Party whose officers have caused damage to any person in the territory of another Contracting Party shall reimburse the latter in full any sums it has paid to the victims or persons entitled on their behalf.

4. Without prejudice to the exercise of its rights vis-à-vis third parties and with the exception of paragraph 3, each Contracting Party shall refrain in the case provided for in paragraph 1 from requesting reimbursement of damages it has sustained from another Contracting Party.

Article 44

1. In accordance with the relevant international agreements and account being taken of local circumstances and technical possibilities, the Contracting Parties shall install, in particular in border areas, telephone, radio, and telex lines and other direct links to facilitate police and customs cooperation, in particular for the timely transmission of information for the purposes of cross-border surveillance and hot pursuit.

2. In addition to these short-term measures, they will in particular consider the following options:

(a) exchanging equipment or posting liaison offers provided with appropriate radio equipment;

(b) widening the frequency bands used in border areas;

(c) establishing common links for police and customs services operating in these same areas;

(d) coordinating their programmes for the procurement of communications equipment, with a view to installing standardised and compatible communications systems.

Article 45

1. The Contracting Parties undertake to adopt the necessary measures in order to ensure that:

(a) the managers of establishments providing accommodation or their agents see to it that aliens accommodated therein, including nationals of the other Contracting Parties and those of other Member States of the European Communities, with the exception of accompanying spouses or accompanying minors or members of travel groups, personally complete and sign registration forms and confirm their identity by producing a valid identity document;

(b) the completed registration forms will be kept for the competent authorities or forwarded to them where such authorities deem this necessary for the prevention of threats, for criminal investigations or for clarifying the circumstances of missing persons or accident victims, save where national law provides otherwise.

2. Paragraph 1 shall apply mutatis mutandis to persons staying in any commercially rented accommodation, in particular tents, caravans and boats.

Article 46[35]

1. In specific cases, each Contracting Party may, in compliance with its national law and without being so requested, send the Contracting Party concerned any information which may be important in helping it combat future crime and prevent offences against or threats to public policy and public security.

2. Information shall be exchanged, without prejudice to the arrangements for cooperation in border areas referred to in Article 39(4), via a central body to be designated. In particularly urgent cases, the exchange of information within the meaning of this Article may take place directly between the police authorities concerned, unless national provisions stipulate otherwise. The central body shall be informed of this as soon as possible.

Article 47

1. The Contracting Parties may conclude bilateral agreements providing for the secondment, for a specified or unspecified period, of liaison officers from one Contracting Party to the police authorities of another Contracting Party.

2. The secondment of liaison officers for a specified or unspecified period is intended to further and accelerate cooperation between the Contracting Parties, particularly by providing assistance:

(a) in the form of the exchange of information for the purposes of combating crime by means of both prevention and law enforcement;

(b) in executing requests for mutual police and judicial assistance in criminal matters;

(c) with the tasks carried out by the authorities responsible for external border surveillance.

3. Liaison officers shall have the task of providing advice and assistance. They shall not be empowered to take independent police action. They shall supply information and perform their duties in accordance with the instructions given to them by the seconding Contracting Party and by the Contracting Party to which they are seconded. They shall report regularly to the head of the police department to which they are seconded.

4. The Contracting Parties may agree within a bilateral or multilateral framework that liaison officers from a Contracting Party seconded to third States shall also represent the interests of one or more other Contracting Parties. Under such agreements, liaison officers seconded to third States shall supply information to other Contracting Parties when requested to do so or on their own initiative and shall, within the limits of their powers, perform duties on behalf of such Parties. The Contracting Parties shall inform one another of their intentions with regard to the secondment of liaison officers to third States.[36]

---

[35] See above FN on Article 39.

[36] Repealed by Council Decision 2003/170/JHA.

CHAPTER 2
MUTUAL ASSISTANCE IN CRIMINAL MATTERS
Article 48

1. The provisions of this Chapter are intended to supplement the European Convention on Mutual Assistance in Criminal Matters of 20 April 1959 as well as, in relations between the Contracting Parties which are members of the Benelux Economic Union, Chapter II of the Benelux Treaty concerning Extradition and Mutual Assistance in Criminal Matters of 27 June 1962, as amended by the Protocol of 11 May 1974, and to facilitate the implementation of those Agreements.

2. Paragraph 1 shall not affect the application of the broader provisions of the bilateral agreements in force between the Contracting Parties.

Article 49
Mutual assistance shall also be afforded:

(a) in proceedings brought by the administrative authorities in respect of acts which are punishable under the national law of one of the two Contracting Parties, or of both, by virtue of being infringements of the rules of law, and where the decision may give rise to proceedings before a court having jurisdiction in particular in criminal matters;[37]

(b) in proceedings for claims for damages arising from wrongful prosecution or conviction;

(c) in clemency proceedings;

(d) in civil actions joined to criminal proceedings, as long as the criminal court has not yet taken a final decision in the criminal proceedings;

(e) in the service of judicial documents relating to the enforcement of a sentence or a preventive measure, the imposition of a fine or the payment of costs for proceedings;

(f) in respect of measures relating to the deferral of delivery or suspension of enforcement of a sentence or a preventive measure, to conditional release or to a stay or interruption of enforcement of a sentence or a preventive measure.

Article 50
(…)[38]

Article 51[39]
The Contracting Parties may not make the admissibility of letters rogatory for search or seizure dependent on conditions other than the following:

---

[37] Lit. a was repealed by Article 2(2) of the Convention on Mutual Assistance in Criminal Matters (MLA Convention), when that Convention came into force (on 23 August 2005).

[38] Article 50 was repealed by Article 8(3) of the Protocol to the Convention on Mutual Assistance in Criminal Matters (MLA Convention) when that Protocol came into force (on 5 October 2005).

[39] **Partially replaced**: Article 51 CISA was partially replaced by the European Investigation Order Directive 2014/41/EU, which. However, Article 34 of that Directive state that it leaves unaffected the possibility for Member States to apply pre-existing instruments (i.e. also Article 51 CISA) in their relations with third countries (i.e. Norway, Iceland, Switzerland and Liechtenstein) as well as in their relations with other Member States not bound by Directive 2014/41 (Denmark and Ireland) (NB: Article 34 of Directive 2014/41/EU is rather **unclear** on the scope of replacement of corresponding CISA provisions, but Article 51 CISA seems envisaged. Moreover the fact that Directive 2014/41/EU is labelled as non-Schengen related poses legal problems).

(a) the act giving rise to the letters rogatory is punishable under the law of both Contracting Parties by a penalty involving deprivation of liberty or a detention order of a maximum period of at least six months, or is punishable under the law of one of the two Contracting Parties by an equivalent penalty and under the law of the other Contracting Party by virtue of being an infringement of the rules of law which is being prosecuted by the administrative authorities, and where the decision may give rise to proceedings before a court having jurisdiction in particular in criminal matters;

(b) execution of the letters rogatory is consistent with the law of the requested Contracting Party.

Article 52

(…)[40]

Article 53

(…)[41]

CHAPTER 3
APPLICATION OF THE NE BIS IN IDEM PRINCIPLE

Article 54

A person whose trial has been finally disposed of in one Contracting Party may not be prosecuted in another Contracting Party for the same acts provided that, if a penalty has been imposed, it has been enforced, is actually in the process of being enforced or can no longer be enforced under the laws of the sentencing Contracting Party.

Article 55

1. A Contracting Party may, when ratifying, accepting or approving this Convention, declare that it is not bound by Article 54 in one or more of the following cases:

(a) where the acts to which the foreign judgment relates took place in whole or in part in its own territory; in the latter case, however, this exception shall not apply if the acts took place in part in the territory of the Contracting Party where the judgment was delivered;

(b) where the acts to which the foreign judgment relates constitute an offence against national security or other equally essential interests of that Contracting Party;

(c) where the acts to which the foreign judgment relates were committed by officials of that Contracting Party in violation of the duties of their office.

2. A Contracting Party which has made a declaration regarding the exception referred to in paragraph 1(b) shall specify the categories of offences to which this exception may apply.

3. A Contracting Party may at any time withdraw a declaration relating to one or more of the exceptions referred to in paragraph 1.

---

[40] Article 52 was repealed by Article 2(2) of the Convention on Mutual Assistance in Criminal Matters (MLA Convention), when that Convention came into force (on 23 August 2005).

[41] Article 53 was repealed by Article 2(2) of the Convention on Mutual Assistance in Criminal Matters (MLA Convention), when that Convention came into force (on 23 August 2005).

4. The exceptions which were the subject of a declaration under paragraph 1 shall not apply where the Contracting Party concerned has, in connection with the same acts, requested the other Contracting Party to bring the prosecution or has granted extradition of the person concerned.

Article 56

If a further prosecution is brought in a Contracting Party against a person whose trial, in respect of the same acts, has been finally disposed of in another Contracting Party, any period of deprivation of liberty served in the latter Contracting Party arising from those acts shall be deducted from any penalty imposed. To the extent permitted by national law, penalties not involving deprivation of liberty shall also be taken into account.

Article 57

1. Where a Contracting Party charges a person with an offence and the competent authorities of that Contracting Party have reason to believe that the charge relates to the same acts as those in respect of which the person's trial has been finally disposed of in another Contracting Party, those authorities shall, if they deem it necessary, request the relevant information from the competent authorities of the Contracting Party in whose territory judgment has already been delivered.

2. The information requested shall be provided as soon as possible and shall be taken into consideration as regards further action to be taken in the proceedings under way.

3. Each Contracting Party shall, when ratifying, accepting or approving this Convention, nominate the authorities authorised to request and receive the information provided for in this Article.

Article 58

The above provisions shall not preclude the application of broader national provisions on the ne bis in idem principle with regard to judicial decisions taken abroad.

CHAPTER 4

EXTRADITION[42]

Article 59

1. The provisions of this chapter are intended to supplement the European Convention on Extradition of 13 September 1957 as well as, in relations between the Contracting Parties which are members of the Benelux Economic Union, Chapter I of the Benelux Treaty concerning Extradition and Mutual

---

[42] Chapter 4 of CISA (Articles 59-66) was **replaced**, from 1 January 2004, by Council Framework Decision 2002/584/JHA on the European arrest warrant. This replacement took effect **only for relations between Member States, but not for relations between Member States and third States** (i.e. Norway, Iceland, Switzerland and Liechtenstein). Article 34(1) of the 2006 Agreement with Iceland and Norway on the surrender procedure between the Member States of the European Union and Iceland and Norway replaced, since its entry into force on 1.11.2019, Chapter 4 of CISA (Articles 59-66) also for relations between Member States and Norway/Iceland.

Assistance in Criminal Matters of 27 June 1962, as amended by the Protocol of 11 May 1974, and to facilitate the implementation of those agreements.

2. Paragraph 1 shall not affect the application of the broader provisions of the bilateral agreements in force between the Contracting Parties.

Article 60[43]

In relations between two Contracting Parties, one of which is not a Party to the European Convention on Extradition of 13 September 1957, the provisions of the said Convention shall apply, subject to the reservations and declarations made at the time of ratifying that Convention or, for Contracting Parties which are not Parties to the Convention, at the time of ratifying, approving or accepting this Convention.

Article 61

(…)[44]

Article 62[45]

1. As regards interruption of limitation of actions, only the provisions of the requesting Contracting Party shall apply.

2. An amnesty granted by the requested Contracting Party shall not prevent extradition unless the offence falls within the jurisdiction of that Contracting Party.

3. The absence of a charge or an official notice authorising proceedings, necessary only under the law of the requested Contracting Party, shall not affect the obligation to extradite.

Article 63

(…)[46]

Article 64

(…)[47]

Article 65

(…)[48]

Article 66[49]

---

[43] According to Council Decision 1999/435/EC it was not considered necessary to determine a legal basis for Article 60 and it was therefore printed in italics in the publication of the Schengen acquis in Official Journal L 239 of 22 September 2000. It had become obsolete, since all Schengen States have become Parties to the 1957 European Convention on Extradition.

[44] According to Article 4(2) of Council Decision 2003/169/JHA, Articles 61, 62(1) and (2), 63 and 65 CISA shall be repealed on the same date that the 1996 Extradition Convention enters into force, which was on 5 November 2019 (see notice concerning entry into force of the 1996 Extradition Convention in OJ C 329, 1.10.2019).

[45] See above FN on Article 61.

[46] See above FN on Article 61.

[47] Article 64 CISA was replaced by Council Decision 2007/533/JHA on the establishment, operation and use of the second generation Schengen Information System (SIS II Decision).

[48] See above FN on Article 61.

[49] According to Article 4(1) of Council Decision 2003/169/JHA, Article 66 CISA shall be repealed on the same date that the 1995 Simplified Extradition Convention enters into force. This was not yet the case.

1. If the extradition of a wanted person is not clearly prohibited under the laws of the requested Contracting Party, that Contracting Party may authorise extradition without formal extradition proceedings, provided that the wanted person agrees thereto in a statement made before a member of the judiciary after being heard by the latter and informed of the right to formal extradition proceedings. The wanted person may be assisted by a lawyer during the hearing.

2. In cases of extradition under paragraph 1, wanted persons who explicitly state that they will relinquish the protection offered by the principle of speciality may not revoke that statement.

CHAPTER 5
TRANSFER OF THE ENFORCEMENT OF CRIMINAL JUDGMENTS[50]

Article 67

The following provisions shall apply between the Contracting Parties which are Parties to the Council of Europe Convention on the Transfer of Sentenced Persons of 21 March 1983, for the purposes of supplementing that Convention.

Article 68

1. The Contracting Party in whose territory a penalty involving deprivation of liberty or a detention order has been imposed by a judgment which has obtained the force of res judicata in respect of a national of another Contracting Party who, by escaping to the national's own country, has avoided the enforcement of that penalty or detention order may request the latter Contracting Party, if the escaped person is within its territory, to take over the enforcement of the penalty or detention order.

2. The requested Contracting Party may, at the request of the requesting Contracting Party, prior to the arrival of the documents supporting the request that the enforcement of the penalty or detention order or part thereof remaining to be served be taken over, and prior to the decision on that request, take the sentenced person into police custody or take other measures to ensure that the person remains within the territory of the requested Contracting Party.

Article 69

The transfer of enforcement under Article 68 shall not require the consent of the person on whom the penalty or the detention order has been imposed. The other provisions of the Council of Europe Convention on the Transfer of Sentenced Persons of 21 March 1983 shall apply mutatis mutandis.

---

[50] According to Article 26(1) of Council Framework Decision 2008/909/JHA on the application of the principle of mutual recognition to judgments in criminal matters imposing custodial sentences or measures involving deprivation of liberty for the purpose of their enforcement in the European Union, the provisions of chapter 5 CISA (Articles 67–69) were **replaced - for relations between Member States, but not for relations between Member States and third States** (i.e. Norway, Iceland, Switzerland and Liechtenstein) - with effect from 5 December 2011.

CHAPTER 6
NARCOTIC DRUGS
Article 70
(...)[51]

Article 71

1. The Contracting Parties undertake as regards the direct or indirect sale of narcotic drugs and psychotropic substances of whatever type, including cannabis, and the possession of such products and substances for sale or export, to adopt in accordance with the existing United Nations Conventions(1), all necessary measures to prevent and punish the illicit trafficking in narcotic drugs and psychotropic substances.

2. The Contracting Parties undertake to prevent and punish by administrative and penal measures the illegal export of narcotic drugs and psychotropic substances, including cannabis, as well as the sale, supply and handing over of such products and substances, without prejudice to the relevant provisions of Articles 74, 75 and 76.

3. To combat the illegal import of narcotic drugs and psychotropic substances, including cannabis, the Contracting Parties shall step up their checks on the movement of persons, goods and means of transport at their external borders. Such measures shall be drawn up by the working party provided for in Article 70. This working party shall consider, inter alia, transferring some of the police and customs staff released from internal border duty and the use of modern drug-detection methods and sniffer dogs.

4. To ensure compliance with this Article, the Contracting Parties shall specifically carry out surveillance of places known to be used for drug trafficking.

5. The Contracting Parties shall do their utmost to prevent and combat the negative effects arising from the illicit demand for narcotic drugs and psychotropic substances of whatever type, including cannabis. Each Contracting Party shall be responsible for the measures adopted to this end.

Article 72

The Contracting Parties shall, in accordance with their constitutions and their national legal systems, ensure that legislation is enacted to enable the seizure and confiscation of the proceeds of the illicit trafficking in narcotic drugs and psychotropic substances.

Article 73
(...)[52]

---

[51] According to Council Decision 1999/435/EC it was not considered necessary to determine a legal basis for Article 70 and it was therefore printed in italics in the publication of the Schengen acquis in Official Journal L 239 of 22 September 2000.

[52] Repealed by Article 2(2) of the Convention on Mutual Assistance in Criminal Matters (MLA Convention), when that Convention came into force (on 23 August 2005).

Article 74
(...)[53]

Article 75

1. As regards the movement of travellers to the territories of the Contracting Parties or their movement within these territories, persons may carry the narcotic drugs and psychotropic substances that are necessary for their medical treatment provided that, at any check, they produce a certificate issued or authenticated by a competent authority of their State of residence.

2. The Executive Committee shall lay down the form and content of the certificate referred to in paragraph 1 and issued by one of the Contracting Parties, with particular reference to details on the nature and quantity of the products and substances and the duration of the journey.

3. The Contracting Parties shall notify each other of the authorities responsible for the issue and authentication of the certificate referred to in paragraph 2.

Article 76

1. The Contracting Parties shall, where necessary, and in accordance with their medical, ethical and practical usage, adopt appropriate measures for the control of narcotic drugs and psychotropic substances which in the territory of one or more Contracting Parties are subject to more rigorous controls than in their own territory, so as not to jeopardise the effectiveness of such controls.

2. Paragraph 1 shall also apply to substances frequently used in the manufacture of narcotic drugs and psychotropic substances.

3. The Contracting Parties shall notify each other of the measures taken in order to monitor the legal trade of the substances referred to in paragraphs 1 and 2.

4. Problems experienced in this area shall be raised regularly in the Executive Committee.

CHAPTER 7
FIREARMS AND AMMUNITION
Article 77-81
(...)[54]

Article 82

The list of arms referred to in Articles 79, 80 and 81 shall not include:

---

[53] According to Council Decision 1999/435/EC it was not considered necessary to determine a legal basis for Article 74 and it was therefore printed in italics in the publication of the Schengen acquis in Official Journal L 239 of 22 September 2000.

[54] According to Council Decision 1999/435/EC it was not considered necessary to determine a legal basis for Articles 77–81 and 83-90 and they were therefore printed in italics in the publication of the Schengen acquis in Official Journal L 239 of 22 September 2000. Footnote 3 of Council Decision 1999/435/EC sets out: *"Articles 77 to 81 and 83 to 90 of the implementing Convention have been replaced by Directive 91/477/EEC on the control of the acquisition and possession of weapons. Weapons of war come within Member States' sphere of competence, under Article 296(1) (b) of the EC Treaty".*

(a) firearms whose model or year of manufacture, save in exceptional cases, predates 1 January 1870, provided that they cannot fire ammunition intended for prohibited arms or arms subject to authorisation;

(b) reproductions of arms listed under (a), provided that they cannot be used to fire metal-case cartridges;

(c) firearms which by technical procedures guaranteed by the stamp of an official body or recognised by such a body have been rendered unfit to fire any kind of ammunition.

Article 83-90

(…)[55]

Article 91

1. The Contracting Parties agree, on the basis of the European Convention on the Control of the Acquisition and Possession of Firearms by Individuals of 28 June 1978, to set up within the framework of their national laws an exchange of information on the acquisition of firearms by persons - whether private individuals or firearms dealers - habitually resident or established in the territory of another Contracting Party. A firearms dealer shall mean any person whose trade or business consists, in whole or in part, in the retailing of firearms.

2. The exchange of information shall concern:

(a) between two Contracting Parties having ratified the Convention referred to in paragraph 1: the firearms listed in Appendix 1(A)(1)(a) to (h) of the said Convention;

(b) between two Contracting Parties at least one of which has not ratified the Convention referred to in paragraph 1: firearms which are subject to authorisation or declaration in each of the Contracting Parties.

3. Information on the acquisition of firearms shall be communicated without delay and shall include the following:

(a) the date of acquisition of the firearm and the identity of the person acquiring it, i.e.:

- in the case of a natural person: surname, forenames, date and place of birth, address and passport or identity card number, date of issue and details of the issuing authority, whether firearms dealer or not,

- in the case of a legal person: the name or business name and registered place of business and the surname, forenames, date and place of birth, address and passport or identity card number of the person authorised to represent the legal person;

(b) the model, manufacturer's number, calibre and other characteristics of the firearm in question and its serial number.

4. Each Contracting Party shall designate the national authority responsible for sending and receiving the information referred to in paragraphs 2 and 3 and shall immediately inform the other Contracting Parties of any change of designated authority.

---

[55] See above FN on Articles 77–81.

5. The authority designated by each Contracting Party may forward the information it has received to the competent local police authorities and the authorities responsible for border surveillance, for the purposes of preventing or prosecuting criminal offences and infringements of rules of law.

TITLE IV
THE SCHENGEN INFORMATION SYSTEM
(…)[56]
TITLE V
TRANSPORT AND MOVEMENT OF GOODS
(…)[57]
TITLE VI
PROTECTION OF PERSONAL DATA[58]
Article 126
1. As regards the automatic processing of personal data communicated pursuant to this Convention, each Contracting Party shall, no later than the date of entry into force of this Convention, adopt the necessary national provisions in order to achieve a level of protection of personal data at least equal to that resulting from the Council of Europe Convention for the Protection of Individuals with regard to Automatic Processing of Personal Data of 28 January 1981.

2. The communication of personal data provided for in this Convention may not take place until the provisions for the protection of personal data as specified in paragraph 1 have entered into force in the territories of the Contracting Parties involved in such communication.

3. In addition, the following provisions shall apply to the automatic processing of personal data communicated pursuant to this Convention:

---

[56] The provisions of Articles 92–119 CISA were replaced by Council Decision 2007/533/JHA on the establishment, operation and use of the second generation Schengen Information System (SIS II Decision), as regards matters falling within the scope of the EU Treaty (*"third pillar" matters*) and by Regulation (EC) No 1987/2006 on the establishment, operation and use of the second generation Schengen Information System (SIS II Regulation), as regards matters falling within the scope of the EC Treaty (*"first pillar" matters*). The replacement took effect on 9.4.2013.

[57] According to Council Decision 1999/435/EC it was not considered necessary to determine a legal basis for Articles 120-125 and they were therefore printed in italics in the publication of the Schengen acquis in Official Journal L 239 of 22 September 2000. Council did not specify the reasons for doing so. In view of the internal market and customs union rules which had been adopted at EC level before 1999, it seems that the reason set out in recital 4(d) of Decision 1999/435/EC was relevant: *"The subject matter of the provision is covered by - and therefore superseded by - existing European Community or Union legislation or by a legal act adopted by all Member States"*.

[58] Articles 126-130 CISA were never formally repealed or replaced. However, these Articles were partially superseded (lex posterior rule) by subsequently adopted EU legislation (the General Data Protection Regulation (EU) 2016/679 and Directive (EU) 2016/680 on the protection of natural persons with regard to the processing of personal data by competent authorities for the purposes of the prevention, investigation, detection or prosecution of criminal offences or the execution of criminal penalties as well as by the predecessors of these legal instruments).

(a) such data may be used by the recipient Contracting Party solely for the purposes for which this Convention stipulates that they may be communicated; such data may be used for other purposes only with the prior authorisation of the Contracting Party communicating the data and in accordance with the law of the recipient Contracting Party; such authorisation may be granted in so far as the national law of the Contracting Party communicating the data so permits;

(b) such data may be used only by the judicial authorities and the departments and authorities carrying out tasks or performing duties in connection with the purposes referred to in paragraph (a);

(c) the Contracting Party communicating such data shall be obliged to ensure the accuracy thereof; should it establish, either on its own initiative or further to a request by the data subject, that data have been provided that are inaccurate or should not have been communicated, the recipient Contracting Party or Parties must be immediately informed thereof; the latter Party or Parties shall be obliged to correct or destroy the data, or to indicate that the data are inaccurate or were unlawfully communicated;

(d) a Contracting Party may not plead that another Contracting Party communicated inaccurate data, in order to avoid its liability under its national law vis-à-vis an injured party; if damages are awarded against the recipient Contracting Party because of its use of inaccurate communicated data, the Contracting Party which communicated the data shall refund in full to the recipient Contracting Party the amount paid in damages;

(e) the transmission and receipt of personal data must be recorded both in the source data file and in the data file in which they are entered;

(f) the joint supervisory authority referred to in Article 115 may, at the request of one of the Contracting Parties, deliver an opinion on the difficulties of implementing and interpreting this Article.

4. This Article shall not apply to the communication of data provided for under Chapter 7 of Title II and Title IV. Paragraph 3 shall not apply to the communication of data provided for under Chapters 2 to 5 of Title III.

Article 127

1. Where personal data are communicated to another Contracting Party pursuant to the provisions of this Convention, Article 126 shall apply to the communication of the data from a non-automated data file and to their inclusion in another non-automated data file.

2. Where, in cases other than those governed by Article 126(1), or paragraph 1 of this Article, personal data are communicated to another Contracting Party pursuant to this Convention, Article 126(3), with the exception of subparagraph (e), shall apply. The following provisions shall also apply:

(a) a written record shall be kept of the transmission and receipt of personal data; this obligation shall not apply where such a record is not necessary given the use of the data, in particular if they are not used or are used only very briefly;

(b) the recipient Contracting Party shall ensure, in the use of communicated data, a level of protection at least equal to that laid down in its national law for the use of similar data;

(c) the decision concerning whether and under what conditions the data subject shall, at his request, be provided information concerning communicated data relating to him shall be governed by the national law of the Contracting Party to which the request was addressed.

3. This Article shall not apply to the communication of data provided for under Chapter 7 of Title II, Chapters 2 to 5 of Title III, and Title IV.

Article 128

1. The communication of personal data provided for by this Convention may not take place until the Contracting Parties involved in that communication have instructed a national supervisory authority to monitor independently that the processing of personal data in data files complies with Articles 126 and 127 and the provisions adopted for their implementation.

2. Where the Contracting Party has, in accordance with its national law, instructed a supervisory authority to monitor independently, in one or more areas, compliance with the provisions on the protection of personal data not entered in a data file, that Contracting Party shall instruct the same authority to supervise compliance with the provisions of this Title in the areas concerned.

3. This Article shall not apply to the communication of data provided for under Chapter 7 of Title II and Chapters 2 to 5 of Title III.

Article 129

As regards the communication of personal data pursuant to Chapter 1 of Title III, the Contracting Parties undertake, without prejudice to Articles 126 and 127, to achieve a level of protection of personal data which complies with the principles of Recommendation No R (87) 15 of 17 September 1987 of the Committee of Ministers of the Council of Europe regulating the use of personal data in the police sector. In addition, as regards the communication of data pursuant to Article 46, the following provisions shall apply:

(a) the data may be used by the recipient Contracting Party solely for the purposes indicated by the Contracting Party which provided the data and in compliance with the conditions laid down by that Contracting Party;

(b) the data may be communicated to police forces and authorities only; data may not be communicated to other authorities without the prior authorisation of the Contracting Party which provided them;

(c) the recipient Contracting Party shall, upon request, inform the Contracting Party which provided the data of the use made of the data and the results thus obtained.

Article 130

If personal data are communicated via a liaison officer as referred to in Article 47 or Article 125, the provisions of this title shall not apply unless the liaison officer communicates such data to the Contracting Party which seconded the officer to the territory of the other Contracting Party.

TITLE VII

EXECUTIVE COMMITTEE
(...)[59]
TITLE VIII
FINAL PROVISIONS
Article 134[60]
The provisions of this Convention shall apply only in so far as they are compatible with Community law.
Article 135[61]
The provisions of this Convention shall apply subject to the provisions of the Geneva Convention relating to the Status of Refugees of 28 July 1951, as amended by the New York Protocol of 31 January 1967.
Article 136[62]
1. A Contracting Party which envisages conducting negotiations on border checks with a third State shall inform the other Contracting Parties thereof in good time.
2. No Contracting Party shall conclude with one or more third States agreements simplifying or abolishing border checks without the prior agreement of the other Contracting Parties, subject to the right of the Member States of the European Communities to conclude such agreements jointly.
3. Paragraph 2 shall not apply to agreements on local border traffic in so far as those agreements comply with the exceptions and arrangements adopted under Article 3(1).
Article 137[63]
This Convention shall not be the subject of any reservations, save for those referred to in Article 60.
Article 138
As regards the French Republic, the provisions of this Convention shall apply only to the European territory of the French Republic.

---

[59] According to Council Decision 1999/435/EC it was not considered necessary to determine a legal basis for Articles 131-133 and they were therefore printed in italics in the publication of the Schengen acquis in Official Journal L 239 of 22 September 2000. Council did not specify the reasons for doing so. It seems that the reason set out in recital 4(c) of Decision 1999/435/EC was relevant: *"The provision relates to institutional rules which are regarded as being superseded by European Union procedures"*.

[60] According to Council Decision 1999/435/EC it was not considered necessary to determine a legal basis for Article 134 and it was therefore printed in italics in the publication of the Schengen acquis in Official Journal L 239 of 22 September 2000. Council did not specify the reasons for doing so. Given the legal effects of the integration of the Schengen acquis into Union law, it seems that the reason set out in recital 4(d) of Decision 1999/435/EC was relevant: *"The subject matter of the provision is covered by - and therefore superseded by - existing European Community or Union legislation or by a legal act adopted by all Member States."*

[61] See above FN on Article 134.

[62] Article 136 was deleted by Article 2(5) of Regulation (EU) No 610/2013.

[63] See above FN on Article 134.

As regards the Kingdom of the Netherlands, the provisions of this Convention shall apply only to the territory of the Kingdom in Europe.

Article 139[64]

1. This Convention shall be subject to ratification, acceptance or approval. The instruments of ratification, acceptance or approval shall be deposited with the Government of the Grand Duchy of Luxembourg, which shall notify all the Contracting Parties thereof.

2. This Convention shall enter into force on the first day of the second month following the deposit of the final instrument of ratification, acceptance or approval. The provisions concerning the setting up, activities and powers of the Executive Committee shall apply as from the entry into force of this Convention. The other provisions shall apply as from the first day of the third month following the entry into force of this Convention.

3. The Government of the Grand Duchy of Luxembourg shall notify all the Contracting Parties of the date of entry into force.

Article 140[65]

1. Any Member State of the European Communities may become a Party to this Convention. Accession shall be the subject of an agreement between that State and the Contracting Parties.

2. Such an agreement shall be subject to ratification, acceptance or approval by the acceding State and by each of the Contracting Parties. It shall enter into force on the first day of the second month following the deposit of the final instrument of ratification, acceptance or approval.

Article 141[66]

1. Any Contracting Party may submit to the depositary a proposal to amend this Convention. The depositary shall forward that proposal to the other Contracting Parties. At the request of one Contracting Party, the Contracting Parties shall re-examine the provisions of the Convention if, in their opinion, there has been a fundamental change in the conditions obtaining when the Convention entered into force.

2. The Contracting Parties shall adopt amendments to this Convention by common consent.

3. Amendments shall enter into force on the first day of the second month following the date of deposit of the final instrument of ratification, acceptance or approval.

Article 142[67]

1. When Conventions are concluded between the Member States of the European Communities with a view to the completion of an area without internal frontiers, the Contracting Parties shall agree on the conditions under which the provisions of this Convention are to be replaced or amended in the light of the corresponding provisions of such Conventions.

---

[64] See above FN on Article 134.
[65] See above FN on Article 134.
[66] See above FN on Article 134.
[67] See above FN on Article 134.

The Contracting Parties shall, to that end, take account of the fact that the provisions of this Convention may provide for more extensive cooperation than that resulting from the provisions of the said Conventions.

Provisions which conflict with those agreed between the Member States of the European Communities shall in any case be adapted.

2. Amendments to this Convention which are deemed necessary by the Contracting Parties shall be subject to ratification, acceptance or approval. The provision contained in Article 141(3) shall apply on the understanding that the amendments will not enter into force before the said Conventions between the Member States of the European Communities enter into force.

Select Cases

Judgment of 21 September 1999, Wijsenbeek (C-378/97, ECR 1999 p. I-6207) ECLI:EU:C:1999:439

Judgment of 18 December 2007, United Kingdom/Council (C-77/05, ECR 2007 p. I-11459) ECLI:EU:C:2007:803

Judgment of 18 December 2007, United Kingdom/Council (C-137/05, ECR 2007 p. I-11593) ECLI:EU:C:2007:805

Judgment of 26 October 2010, United Kingdom/Council (C-482/08, ECR 2010 p. I-10413) ECLI:EU:C:2010:631

Judgment of 22 June 2010, Melki and Abdeli (C-188/10 and C-189/10, ECR 2010 p. I-5667) ECLI:EU:C:2010:363

Judgment of 19 July 2012, Adil (C-278/12 PPU) ECLI:EU:C:2012:508

Judgment of 7 March 2017, X and X (C-638/16 PPU) ECLI:EU:C:2017:173

Judgment of 19 March 2019, Arib and others (C-444/17) ECLI:EU:C:2019:220

Judgment of 21 March 2024, Landeshauptstadt Wiesbaden (C-61/22) ECLI:EU:C:2024:251

Terminology

Decision 1999/437/EC Council Decision of 17 May 1999 on certain arrangements for the application of the Agreement concluded by the Council of the European Union and the Republic of Iceland and the Kingdom of Norway concerning the association of those two States with the implementation, application and development of the Schengen acquis; OJ L 176, 10.7.1999, pp. 31–33.

Denmark Protocol Protocol (No 5) on the position of Denmark (1997) as amended in 2009 by Protocol 1 to the Treaty of Lisbon. Consolidated version: Protocol (No 22) on the position of Denmark.

Liechtenstein Schengen Association Protocol Protocol between the European Union, the European Community, the Swiss Confederation, and the Principality of Liechtenstein on the accession of the Principality of Liechtenstein to the Agreement between the European Union, the European Community and the Swiss Confederation on the Swiss Confederation's association with the implementation, application, and development of the Schengen acquis; OJ L 160, 18.6.2011, pp. 3–18.

Norway/Iceland Schengen Association Agreement Agreement concluded by the Council of the European Union and the Republic of Iceland and the Kingdom of Norway concerning the latter's' association with the implementation, application, and development of the Schengen acquis; OJ L 176, 10.7.1999 pp. 36–62.

(Schengen Acquis Determination) Decision 1999/435/EC Council Decision of 20 May 1999 concerning the definition of the Schengen acquis for the purpose of determining, in conformity with the relevant provisions of the Treaty establishing the European Community and the Treaty on European Union, the legal basis for each of the provisions or decisions which constitute the acquis; OJ L 176, 10.7.1999, pp. 1–16.

Schengen Protocol Protocol (No 2) integrating the Schengen acquis into the framework of the European Union (1997) as amended in 2009 by Protocol 1 to the Treaty of Lisbon. Consolidated version: Protocol (No 19) on the Schengen acquis integrated into the framework of the European Union (OJ C 326, 26.10.2012, pp. 290–292).

Swiss Schengen Association Agreement Agreement between the European Union, the European Community and the Swiss Confederation on the Swiss Confederation's association with the implementation, application, and development of the Schengen acquis; OJ L 53, 27.2.2008, pp. 52–79.

UK/Ireland Protocol Protocol (No 4) on the position of the United Kingdom and Ireland (1997) as amended in 2009 by Protocol 1 to the Treaty of Lisbon. Consolidated version: Protocol (No 21) on the position of the United Kingdom and Ireland in respect of the area of freedom, security, and justice.

(Ventilation) Decision 1999/436/EC Council Decision of 20 May 1999 determining, in conformity with the relevant provisions of the Treaty establishing the European Community and the Treaty on European Union, the legal basis for each of the provisions or decisions which constitute the Schengen acquis; OJ L 176, 10.7.1999, pp. 17–30.

SPRINGER NATURE

GPSR Compliance

The European Union's (EU) General Product Safety Regulation (GPSR) is a set of rules that requires consumer products to be safe and our obligations to ensure this.

If you have any concerns about our products, you can contact us on ProductSafety@springernature.com

In case Publisher is established outside the EU, the EU authorized representative is:

Springer Nature Customer Service Center GmbH
Europaplatz 3
69115 Heidelberg, Germany

The manufacturer's authorised representative in the EU is Springer Nature Customer Service Centre GmbH, Europaplatz 3, 69115 Heidelberg, Germany. If you have any concerns regarding our products, please contact ProductSafety@springernature.com

Printed and bound by CPI Group (UK) Ltd, Croydon, CR0 4YY

01/12/2025
02008619-0006